First published in Great Britain in 2024 by
Biteback Publishing Ltd, London
Copyright © Tina Shingler 2024

ISBN 978-1-78590-901-6

10 9 8 7 6 5 4 3 2 1

A CIP catalogue record for this book is available from the British Library.

Set in Adobe Caslon Pro

Printed and bound in Great Britain by
CPI Group (UK) Ltd, Croydon CR0 4YY

FSC
www.fsc.org
MIX
Paper | Supporting
responsible forestry
FSC® C171272

TINA SHINGLER

# HAIR APPARENT

## A VOYAGE AROUND MY ROOTS

Biteback Publishing

*To Chloe and Felix Mills,*
*May you always blossom where you are planted*

*'You can never cross the ocean unless you have the courage to lose sight of the shore'*

CHRISTOPHER COLUMBUS

# CONTENTS

# PREFACE

I grew up a Black Barnardo's child in the '50s and '60s and at three years old, official records show that I was 'boarded out' into the foster care of a white, working-class family in a rural community in Yorkshire. I was one of the lucky ones, bypassing the dead hand of institutional care for the comfort of a regular family. My foster family was not regular by any stretch, but they were kind and caring and that was more than enough; more than an unwanted Black kid had any right to expect, some uncharitable voices were quick to say. With Barnardo's as my constant overseer, I was expected to reflect their Christian values and so I was hastily baptised by my new foster family and began to attend Sunday school regularly. From my earliest days as a hi-vis outlier, I knew that I had a job to do: I must do everything possible to fit in. While it was clear that I was never going to blend naturally into my surroundings, I must at least try to 'normalise' my Black self within the small-town parameters. My mission was simple: to be as good as gold and to be no trouble to anyone. The alternative was all too real. The fear of being sent back into the anonymity of institutional care hovered over my childhood like the sword of Damocles.

Whenever I came home from school and saw the familiar car of the Barnardo's visitor parked outside the gate, I'd get an anxious twinge. The little Morris Minor belonged to Miss F, who I knew was here to file a full report on me back to the Barnardo's Mothership. This middle-aged lady was kindly enough, but I knew she was here to probe my foster parents and then me about my merits, misdemeanours and character flaws. Miss F's regular visits were a constant reminder of my privileged status in a proper family; a status that must be earned and that could be revoked at any time. She was the ultimate deterrent to behaving badly, and knowing my status was conditional felt like being on indefinite probation.

While emotionally, I could always go into hiding, physically, there was nowhere to run. I was out there in plain sight: the Black kid with the crazy mop of hair. More than my hi-vis skin tone, it was the strange texture of my hair that was a talking point, and more often than I liked, it was a touching point too. My hair was quite literally up for grabs, as adults and children alike felt free to tug and poke at it with curiosity. From their scornful looks and comments, I began to understand that my hair was an unruly beast and trying to tame it was as much a public service as a personal pressure.

So, growing up in the '60s as a Black face in a white space, I always knew that my well-being was conditional, even precarious. Popular British TV comedies of the time reminded me of this with their unapologetic derision of 'wogs', 'coons' and 'fuzzy-wuzzies'. Meanwhile, prime-time Saturday night viewing was *The Black and White Minstrel Show*, where white men got up in blackface and woolly little wigs, sang and danced with leggy white girls in a wonderland of showbiz glamour and sparkle. What to make of it? These were confusing signals for a lone Black girl swimming in white waters. I learned that faking being Black was high entertainment and jolly good fun for all the family. But as the Conservative MP Enoch Powell reminded us in his famous 'Rivers of Blood' speech in 1968, nobody likes the real thing. The vocal anti-immigration lobby made no fine distinctions between a newly arrived Black population and those born in Britain who knew no other country, no other reality. We were all the same colour, weren't we? We weren't welcome and we should all go back to where we came from. And in my little corner of the world where White Was Always Right, the message I received loud and clear was that while I might be allowed onto the boat, I had better not start making any damn waves by rocking it.

Many young Black people are now growing up confident in the power of their naturally kinky hair and all its amazing transmutations. As well as inspiring endless artistic and creative interpretations, its shapeshifting properties allow them to continually reinvent themselves. By resisting the use of harsh chemicals to alter its texture, their hair projects a sense of pride and a belief in their natural beauty. They get it. They always did. They understand its language and they have learned to express their personalities through the myriad of inventive styles its peculiar strength and density inspires. For them, I hope that these pages will be a recognition and a celebration of what they already know: that they have springing out of their scalps something so electrifying, so complex and so terrifically versatile and beautiful that it's like having an extra gear not just to their look but to their whole personality.

But alas, it wasn't always so. History has not always allowed earlier generations of Black women to take a rightful pride and joy in their natural Afro hair, and their 'hairstories' have been ambivalent ones. The intricate texture of their hair has been weighed down with social and political history in every kinky curl. For years, the pressure to conform to a 'white norm' has skewed their vision of their natural beauty and led them to undervalue one of our most outstanding physical assets.

It's a pressure that has been ingrained since childhood and it's followed us into the classroom, the workplace and our most intimate relationships in adulthood. In our relentless efforts to 'unkink' our hair, we have overheated it with powerful dryers, hot combs and straightening tongs, literally scorching and sizzling the life out of it. We have chemically 'relaxed' it again and again, exposing ourselves to toxins that we now know to have damaging effects not only to our hair but potentially to our long-term health as a whole. The war to convert our hair to what we've been led to believe is the True Way, the White Way, has been a holy crusade fought with righteous determination and aided with evermore ingenious weaponry created by the big pharmaceutical and cosmetic companies. In the process, we've caused untold physical damage to ourselves while chipping away at our self-esteem.

This relentless sense of feeling 'less than' has been exacerbated for those of us who, for whatever reason, were forced to live our Black experience in isolation from Black communities. Our hairstories have often taken us on a long and lonely road trip towards self-acceptance and we have struggled to fully appreciate the amazing properties of the natural texture of our hair. Overwhelmed by the complexity of its texture, we were at a loss as to how to care for it practically and emotionally.

We displaced Black girls inherited none of the nifty braiding skills and intensive haircare rituals that Black women pass on as a matter of course to the younger generation – rituals embedded in earliest memories and which connect us to tradition, family and a sense of belonging. When we looked to see who was behind us, who we could learn from, there was no one there. We had no role models, no one to emulate or to guide us. We lacked the cultural confidence to view our hair with anything but the alarm and dismay we saw in the white eyes of our carers and those around us. Our only inheritance was frustration and an unspoken sense of shame. It's as if we were missing a vital key to our identity right from the start.

In absorbing this white angst around our hair, we've felt little love for it and, by default, little love for ourselves. We've grown up hearing the words 'frizzy', 'bushy', 'wiry', 'unmanageable' and 'impenetrable' and we've accepted them because there's been no one around to tell us otherwise. With no one to teach us the basics of Black haircare or the loving patience needed to manage it properly, our relationship with our springy, often intractable curls has been a combative one. In the process, there's been a sense of something lost, personally and culturally.

I like to think that, despite getting off to a bad start

with it, I've 'grown into' my hair now and I'm able to appreciate and enjoy its incredible versatility. Just knowing that this complex network of twisted coils springing from my scalp links my DNA to generations of Black women near and far, and to their extraordinary tales of survival, strength and creative genius, is a terrific inspiration. It has helped me understand myself better, forge my own identity and create a sense of my own worth better than any self-improvement manual.

Over the years, in my writing, I've made random references to the challenging texture of my hair and people's responses to it; the good, the bad and the downright ugly. It was only when I began patching some of these extracts together that I realised I'd got not only some compelling hair adventures but a personal 'hairmoir' spanning several countries and more than seven decades of social, political and cultural change. This seemed like something worth developing and maybe even sharing. Before I knew it, I was writing a personal manifesto of survival, resilience and identity, as I unravelled my own lifetime's relationship with my hair. Testing the waters, I created a presentation around it with photos and musical extracts and took it into schools, businesses, libraries and local arts festivals. Vibrant feedback from audiences both Black and white sparked conversations on everything from racial justice, politics and social history to feminism, self-esteem and the thrilling power of creativity. It was these waves of positive energy that powered the writing of this book.

You can spend your whole life trying not to rock that blasted boat. You hold steady as you navigate the dangerous shallows and rocky outcrops, and all the time, without really knowing it, you are quietly going under. You are drowning a little inside. Then, one day, you decide maybe you'll build your own boat. You'll build it to your own specifications and you'll set your own course. Like most adventures, it's scary at first, but you're free and sailing solo. You're ready to revisit some familiar places and maybe discover some new ones along the way. You've finally got a clear view all the way to the horizon.

*'This too I have learned from the river: everything returns'*
*SIDDHARTHA*, HERMANN HESSE

# CHAPTER ONE

# AFTER THE TAJ

Long before the Beatles were getting their minds blown by the Maharishi Mahesh Yogi, I had my own ideas about India. From the moment I discovered the *National Geographic* collection in the school library, I was drawn to its powerful mystique. India was where the mighty Himalayas gouged clouds with a remote, cold beauty. It was a country crammed with Mogul forts and palaces, Hindu temples, mosques and teeming, ramshackle old cities tumbling down to the banks of the sacred Ganges. But it was in 1968, when we saw those first pictures of the 'Fab Four' bedecked with flowery garlands sitting at the feet of their guru, that India entered world consciousness as a place of deep mysticism and spiritual awakening. Those pictures captured the 'wild child' spirit of the late '60s with its hippy-trippy slogans of 'Turn on, tune in and drop out' and 'Make Love Not War'. All at once India was the 'hip' place to be and Transcendental Meditation or 'TM' was the 'groovy' thing to do. Sitting cross-legged like preschoolers with their benign-looking yogi, the Beatles were smiling, portraying an air of hopeful innocence. Gone were the famous smirks and cheeky grins. They looked becalmed, receptive. In India, they were ready to relearn themselves. And they made it look so easy, we were more than willing to believe it. Peace be the journey.

But even if I'd had the makings of a hippy, at fourteen, I was still too young to pack my bags and head east in search of enlightenment. I had homework and hockey practice to worry about. So, like everyone else, I settled for wearing a lot of cheesecloth with strings of 'love beads' and reading Hermann Hesse's *Siddhartha*, the spiritual handbook of the '60s. My road to self-discovery would have to be put on hold for a few more years, or at least until I'd finished school. But just wait, I promised my teenage self; one day I'll have my own spiritual journey, see if I don't.

Like *Siddhartha*'s river of many voices, the years went slipping by, sometimes in a noisy babble and sometimes in a murmur. I grew up, went to university, lived and worked in both Italy and the US for many years. I married and had a dazzling daughter. Life began to squeeze, with the demands of work, family and relationships gobbling up all my energy. Opting out to 'find myself' in India, or anywhere else on the planet, became the stuff of idle, youthful, even selfish, fantasy.

It would be more than thirty years after the Beatles' inspirational journey east that the stars aligned for me with India.

By then, I had been working as a government press officer in Yorkshire for more than ten years. Writing press notices and media plans, rallying journalists, meeting and briefing government ministers, I was doing the bidding of Whitehall departments 'up north'. Now I was a fiercely independent, middle-aged single parent, which meant my daughter and I were entirely reliant on my salary alone. I was lucky. It wasn't such a bad salary, but it had to go a long way and it was often a struggle. I wasn't unhappy. I had a decent job, great friends and a terrific kid, but there was a nagging sense of lack within me; a feeling of being hopelessly 'stuck' in my own life. Like the computer screen I stared into for several hours every day, I longed to be refreshed, maybe entirely rebooted.

So when my church congregation announced a tour of the sacred sites of northern India, it was as if a long-lost prayer were being answered; a reminder to keep faith with past dreams and aspirations. Just reading the proposed itinerary gave me a rush of excitement. I could already feel something inside me beginning to shift. There were visits to a Buddhist monastery, Hindu temples, mosques, the Taj Mahal and the Sikh Golden Temple at Amritsar. Just the thought of India felt like the first cool drops of rain on my parched soul. India would unlock me. It would free whatever it was that felt trapped inside me – hope, ambition, inspiration, passion? So far it had no name, no voice and no shape.

It had been a long time coming, but this, I told myself, was my moment. Surely I'd earned this.

India would transform me; I was certain of it. I would come back different. I would be chilled out and destressed. I might even take up yoga and meditation; maybe get a taste for brown rice and mung beans. I remembered the Beatles with the Maharishi and their cosmic smiles. All these years later, of course, the world was less naive; we now know those pictures had been carefully curated for the international press and that behind the Maharishi's benevolent smile was a man on the make. But whatever had happened to the Beatles in India, it had changed the direction of their music and their lives. Now it was my turn.

*Siddhartha*'s river was calling me and I was ready to listen.

India wallops your senses. Nothing prepares you for the staggering assault of its noise, its smells and its scalding colours; they swamp you, swallowing you up like a tidal wave. Take a rickshaw ride through the rollicking chaos of downtown New Delhi and you feel as if, before coming to India, you've been sleepwalking through life. You've been sleepwalking in a monochrome world with the volume turned down.

The heat may hang heavy as a damp blanket, but underneath it I'm feeling as stripped and raw as a freshly peeled prawn. My pores are wide open, my senses tingling. I mean to suck up every moment of this experience. I'm ready to let India happen to me.

Like the rest of the group, I was overwhelmed by the strange newness of everything I was seeing and feeling. A big part of this was getting used to the clinging entourage of beggars that all tourists acquire in India. We had only to step off the coach and we were besieged and then aggressively pursued. Our Indian guides cut a swathe through them, swatting them off like flies with what seemed to us a callous indifference. But, running the gauntlet of those imploring faces, pitiful pleas and outstretched hands, it was hard to pretend that these wretched souls were no more than a minor inconvenience to be navigated.

Reading and hearing about the poverty in India is one thing, but seeing the everyday reality of desperate and grinding deprivation was an almighty shock. It was a sickening moral dilemma. Give to one and be mobbed by all of them; or follow the lead of our guides and slice through them like a Swiss Army blade, looking neither to left nor right. It was a lot to take in; compassion and guilt battling with our natural alarm and fear of being set upon.

So it was a while before I noticed that alongside the gangs of beggars who followed us all, I was attracting a separate little posse of hangers-on, a splinter group who only had eyes for me.

'I see you've got another fan club,' said one of my fellow travellers as we all stood outside the magnificent Red Fort in Delhi while the guide negotiated our entrance.

He nodded towards a rag-tag bunch of street kids who had been trailing us from the coach park. They now stood off at distance, jabbing fingers in my direction and hooting with laughter. I shrugged and forced an amiable smile that belied how unnerving I found their attentions.

The truth is this kept happening. These kids would spring up everywhere, running alongside me in twos and threes until their excited jabber and laughter recruited others. God alone knew what they were saying, but it was clear that I'd been singled out as a figure of fun. Now, I've never minded people having a laugh at my expense. In fact, over the years I've become a master in the art of self-deprecation, especially if the payoff was a laugh all round. But these kids were laughing right in my face. These kids were jeering at me. Apparently, I was an absolute hoot. It was hard to make light of the relentless harassment that made me feel so awkward and freakish. To save face, I pretended to share the good-natured bemusement of the rest of my group. *Kids, eh? What can you do?* But in reality, I was embarrassed and confused. What did they want? Why couldn't they leave me alone? I couldn't seem to shake them off. My role as a reluctant Pied Piper was becoming a damn nuisance.

At first, I was mystified. I just didn't get it. True, as the only Black person I definitely stood out in our small British party. But so what? You only had to look around to see that a lot of Indian people – including most of these tormenting kids – were a *whole lot blacker* than I was. So what the hell was the joke? Then it hit me. Of course, it wasn't me they were guffawing at. It was my hair. These Indian kids had never seen anything like it. It was my natural kinky hair that had them in stitches. What the hell was that springy stuff standing out on top of my head? Whatever it was, it was *hilarious*. I was a walking comedy act.

I was mortified and I was angry. *Remember, they're just kids*, I told myself in an effort to claw back some perspective. *They're doing what kids do. They're poking fun at something unusual. And here in India, it just happens to be you and your head of hair. Get a grip and keep your cool.*

I thought back to my own daughter in her pre-teen years. How she would pester and harangue me with repetitive demands about sleepovers, new shoes or upping her pocket money.

'For heaven's sake, will you *stop* annoying me!' I would plead.

'I'm a kid. That's my job,' she would answer, without missing a beat.

These Indian kids were only doing their job. Doing what came naturally. They were annoying all right, but to them I had a comical head of hair that was pure entertainment. I was the funny woman with stand-up hair. Still, it felt like a kind of persecution, although they could have no idea of how humiliating I found their attentions, how embarrassed it made me feel in front of the rest of the group I was travelling with. But I was all grown up and I wasn't about to let a bunch of feral kids get to me, was I? India was a once-in-a-lifetime experience for me. I was on a spiritual journey here, a quest for deeper meaning.

*All you have to do is ignore them*, I told myself as I tried to quiet their mocking jibes with some of the meditation techniques I'd been reading up on.

*Just breathe. Be the calm you are seeking. Choose stillness in the midst of movement and chaos.*

Then we arrived at the Taj Mahal.

Like Mickey Mouse is to America, the Taj Mahal is everyone's quick cultural reference to India. But no matter how many times you've seen it in books, travelogues and on TV, nothing comes close to the moment you step through the great arched gateway and get your first breathless glimpse of its dream-like sublimity. There are no superlatives. At first sight, I remember being afraid to blink in case it simply evaporated like the shimmering mirage it seemed to be.

*It* didn't evaporate, of course, but I very soon wished that *I* could.

On either side of the long reflecting pool leading up to the Taj, all I could see were droves of kids being herded about by their teachers. In their crisp school uniforms and in orderly crocodile formation, these children were a world away from the ragamuffins on the streets of New Delhi. They were middle-class kids on a school trip to their country's most iconic monument and they were under strict supervision. Just look how the teachers were keeping them in line.

Translucent and glowing like a magnificent opal in the morning sun, the Taj lay before me; but even as I tried to draw on its cool and timeless serenity, part of me was fighting the urge to head back to the sanctuary of the coach.

For once in India, I was glad of the crowds. There were people surging everywhere in and around the grounds of the Taj. Like a tiger in the long grass, I hoped I'd be able to conceal myself more easily.

But once the first sharp-eyed kid spotted me, it was open season. After being drilled about the history of the great Mogul dynasty, the architectural symmetry and splendour of the Taj and the tragic love story behind its creation, here at last was the light entertainment. Bring on the clowns. Me and my frizzy mop were the comic relief. Now, as each school group alerted the next, all eyes shot in my direction and a wave of shrieks and giggles rippled down the line like an electric charge. Teachers, barely concealing their own mirth when they saw me, were struggling to keep order in the ranks.

So much for cool serenity; I felt grotesque, ridiculous. I was the bearded lady, the freakshow.

I had no control over the kids' reactions; all I could do was try to manage my own. Rising above it and pretending not to be bothered seemed the only dignified option. I tried to take refuge in irony. Imagine, these kids had come from all over India to marvel at one of the most breathtaking monuments in the world; this was their stupendous heritage. Yet here they were goggling and pointing fingers at the woman with the weird hair. Hard as it was to believe, my wiry curls were threatening to upstage the Taj Mahal.

It was meant to be the high point of the whole trip, but for me the Taj Mahal marked a 'before' and 'after' in India. After the Taj, I was desperate to keep my hair in hiding. The first chance I got, I went out and bought a lot of cheap silk scarves and pashminas. It was time to get inventive. I devised a colourful range of head wraps and turbans, twisting and tying them into elaborate styles, anything to hide my laughable head of hair. I'd often enjoyed wearing head wraps as a fashion choice, but in India it felt like an urgent cover-up. It was as if I were hiding a shameful secret, a deformity that must be kept out of sight at all costs. After the Taj, I covered my head *all the time* in India. My hair was turning out to be too damn sensational. It was provoking too much unwanted attention and it was seriously hampering the path on my spiritual journey.

# CHAPTER TWO

# GROWING UP
# WITH GOLLY

With my hair under wraps, I drew no more attention in India than any other tourist. Visiting the
temples, mosques and holy shrines, I merged back into the
group again and I no longer felt like I was heading up a
circus parade with a riotous band of followers at my heels.
Now, instead of just moving about in India, I could begin
to let India move in me. What didn't change, however,
were the thrusting gangs of beggars who sprang up wherever we went. But after our first encounters with them,
when we'd recoiled from their determined assaults, it was
surprising how quickly we got used to them. They were
part of the Indian landscape, inevitable and unavoidable.
When we could, we gave, but most of the time it was impossible without inciting a mob scene. Instead, setting our

eyes on the middle distance, we learned to move our way through them.

Perched in the foothills of the Himalayas, the Buddhist monastery at Dharamshala has ravishing views into deep-wooded valleys that swoop up to colossal snow-capped peaks. The red-robed monks glide about with ineffable calm under strings of bright prayer flags that flutter and snap in the mountain breeze. The waft of incense is everywhere. In the cool innards of the temple, the monks' hypnotic chanting evokes an overwhelming sense of peace and harmony that seems to still the soul. Surely, if ever there was a time and place to get right with your inner rhythms, this was it. Yet for all the transcendent atmosphere of Dharamshala, I felt more like a journalist, observing and taking notes, than a pilgrim on a spiritual quest. Try as I might, I couldn't seem to plug into the prayerful aura around me. It was as if my spiritual wick had been dampened. It refused to be lit.

The pestering kids were gone now, but I could still hear their gleeful mockery. I had let them get under my skin, and now their shrieks of taunting laughter were permanently in my head like an annoying earworm. They had kicked open a door into my childhood and the past now roared into the present with a storm of memories.

I was the little 'coloured' girl again in an all-white rural community in Yorkshire; the little misfit 'half-caste' with the strange mop of frizzy hair who always kept my head down because I never knew when I might come under fire. It could happen anywhere, in the schoolyard, on the street, in the playground by the swings. Often, I could see it coming and I would brace myself for impact, but it could just as easily be a stealth attack catching me off guard, sudden and ruthless. All I knew was that once I left the shelter of my foster home, there were no safety zones. It could be *this* kid walking towards me who would harass me, or the abuse could come from *that* kid at the top of the street. Then there were those lads from the local housing estate who never missed an opportunity for a potshot. I was such an obvious, irresistible target. I was asking for it. And it was always the same sneering words spat out like bullets: 'NigNog', 'Blackie', 'Wog', 'Coon' and sometimes, like the *coup de grâce*, the full stinging force of the 'N-word'.

In general, there wasn't much call for this kind of language in small-town North Yorkshire, so these words, that I only ever heard around myself and my foster sister, seemed to hold an added relish for our tormentors.

But just as often it was the more benign 'Fuzzy-wuzzy', 'Mophead' or, in the broadest Yorkshire dialect, 'Gerraway, you don't call that stuff *'air*, do you?'

All this time and I'd thought the wounds had scarred over; but from Delhi to Dharamshala, scenes I thought long forgotten were surfacing again. That lone little Black girl was still with me. And so was her hair; and even after all these years, it still had the power to diminish me.

Growing up in a white foster home in an all-white community, I found that my hair's unusual texture was met with curiosity and often with outright derision: 'Here, let's have a feel of it' and 'How on earth do you comb *that stuff?*' or 'What kind of shampoo do you use? Is it the stuff they use to clean carpets or what?'

My hair didn't behave like regular hair. It didn't grow down; it grew out. It wasn't loose, so it didn't blow about in the breeze or fall into my eyes. In fact, it didn't move at all. It was static. I got so used to people making fun of it that I too could only think of it in terms of a joke; a joke that I couldn't bring myself to laugh about.

There's a photograph of me at four years old posing with my Black foster sister. Together we were pretty much the entire Black population of the small market town where we grew up. And yes, shocking as it might seem today, we *are* dressed up as golliwogs. It was the annual fancy dress parade and this was our white foster mother's idea of 'working with what you've got'. And what we had got was our dark skin and crazy fuzzy hair. What we had got was that we were golly look-alikes.

But don't think for a moment we were random golliwogs.

We were the Robertson's Golden and Silver Shred gollies straight off the jam jars. In fact, a closer look at the photo reveals we have oranges and lemons in our little baskets and we are proudly sporting our golly badges. For those who won't remember, the badges were an early version of the loyalty card; the idea being that you got a 'free' enamel badge when you had collected so many golly labels from the back of enough marmalade jars. The infectious TV jingle urged us to keep our eyes peeled for the golly. And we did. We all did. In his familiar royal blue tailcoat and red bow tie, the Robertson's golly mascot was a phenomenal advertising success that was first dreamed up in 1928. More than 20 million golly badges were distributed across Britain before he was finally 'retired' in 2001. I know! 2001, you say. That's how long it took advertisers to recognise that the racial undertones of the mascot were no longer appropriate in Britain's fast-changing demographic; that maybe, just maybe, a pop-eyed, grinning and capering Black minstrel selling their jam products wasn't considered that cute any more. You think?

Be that as it may, back in the 1960s Robertson's golly reigned supreme. The jolly little fellow was a household favourite who was instantly recognisable everywhere. So I can't help feeling that Mary, our foster mother, knew she was onto a winner as she knocked up our little golly suits on her old Singer sewing machine. We were such a safe bet. Not one but *two* little Black girls got up as the famous jam-jar gollies. We were naturals (no boot polish required). We were sure to turn heads and very likely to win prizes.

Some of the entrants in the fancy dress parade that year felt robbed as there was no third prize. The two Robertson's gollies swept the competition off the board and came in joint first. I seem to remember that Little Bo-Peep, with bonnet and shepherd's staff, wept inconsolably, while the Lone Ranger was too busy 'shooting' imaginary 'Injuns' to care. As for the winners, well, there they stand in front of the sweet pea canes in the garden, and I just thank God we were both still too young to get the joke.

There was a time when I used to have a lot of trouble looking at that photo. Apart from the implicit irony of the picture, then and now, I recognise that little girl with her costume slightly askew. I know her. There's no getting away from her. She's wary, uncertain and camera-shy. She's tired of always being looked at, always noticed and remarked upon. And she's already taking refuge in books to escape from prying eyes and questions. Reading, I was discovering, was a good get-out for not engaging with people. With my head, quite literally, in a book, I was more likely to be left alone or overlooked. Unlike my foster sister, who was a year older and more easy-going, smiling at the camera didn't and still doesn't come naturally to me.

Like most women of her generation, Mary was an accomplished seamstress and it's easy to see that she took a lot of trouble making our costumes. But what leaves a real impression in the photo is the state of our hair. Sticking up in matted clumps, it looks not so much unkempt as utterly unloved. I don't know about my foster sister, but even at this early age, I'm pretty sure that I was already suffering from acute hair-anxiety. All the photos from around this time tell the same unhappy hair story.

But if our hair was neglected, it wasn't for want of trying on Mary's part. She did her best, but what did a white working-class housewife know about managing the complex texture of hair like ours? How could she have any idea of how to manage such alien stuff? But as a practical, down-to-earth Yorkshire woman, Mary nevertheless rolled up her sleeves with every intention of 'fettling' it.

Fettle: it's a good, solid word, isn't it? The *Oxford English Dictionary* gives a whole list of meanings for it, from its modern industrial applications to more idiomatic usages such as the Middle English 'to address oneself to battle'. In other words, it's fighting talk, and when used in Yorkshire dialect, it usually means 'to sort something out once and for all'.

And so our hair became Mary's personal battlefield, and her valiant attempts at 'fettling' it were distressing and painful ordeals that we dreaded. Brushes and combs became instruments of torture that tore into our hair, only to be instantly snarled up in the impenetrable tight tangle of coiled curls. The complex texture of our hair proved resistant to bristles of brushes and it gave no quarter to flimsy combs, bending and sometimes snapping them clean in two. Mary tugged and teased in vain while we sobbed and squirmed in misery. It felt as if we were having our hair ripped out at the roots. Distressed by our suffering and exhausted by her futile efforts, Mary did the only thing she could. Our so-called hair was not going to get the better of *her*, so she reached for the scissors.

Like Marie Antoinette at the guillotine, we took it in turns to kneel with our head in Mary's lap and wait for the chop. Then it was yank and snip, yank and snip as she cropped our hair close to the scalp as evenly as she could. Being unceremoniously shorn like sheep every so often felt like a punishment. It served us right for having such troublesome hair. Back then, it was common for little boys to have their hair close-cropped but not the girls. Looking boyish was an added indignity.

When I looked around at the girls in my class at primary school, I knew that *their* hair didn't cause them this kind of stress – and why should it? With their loose, free-flowing locks, there was no need for them to flinch at the sight of a hairbrush. Their mothers had already instilled in them a sense of pride about their hair, adorning it with pretty ribbons, slides and hairbands and encouraging them to take good care of it. Brushes and combs were not their enemy, they were simply essential grooming tools. I would watch girls slowly drawing a comb through their hair, with dreamy, half-closed eyes, as if in a trance. It looked like a soothing, relaxing operation and a long way from my own tearful hair-wrangling with brushes and combs. It was as if my classmates already knew that their hair was going to be one of their best assets, that it was a big part of being pretty. And isn't that what every little girl wanted?

When I was out at the local shops with Mary, I was back in the firing line. No longer able to hide behind my books, I dreaded being waylaid by one of her gossipy friends. These stout, 'I-speak-as-I-find', Yorkshire women were a frightening breed. Broad-shouldered and tight-lipped with judgement, they looked at Mary, shaking their heads with a kind of baffled pity.

'Of all the kiddies who need a good home, you had to get yourself a couple of little darkies,' one of them said to her with sanctimonious indignation.

Determined to have their say, they were just as determined to have their feel. Without reference to either Mary or myself, they proceeded to dig their fingers into my hair for a good old-fashioned rummage, tugging and twisting the dense curls and examining the texture between thumb and forefinger. It seemed to repel and fascinate them at the same time and they shook their heads ruefully at Mary. If she was struggling with it, they had little sympathy. It served her right for taking us on when there were surely more deserving (white) kids she could have lavished her attention on.

'Ooh, it is queer stuff, i'nt it? Feels just like wire wool. However do you manage it, luv?' they gloated.

I hated those nosy old crows with all their poking and probing and their curdling looks; but I knew they weren't wrong. Without proper care and attention, my hair was as coarse as rush matting. And they were right again: it was 'queer stuff'. I could scarcely bear to touch it myself. I didn't want anything to do with it. And if I had no respect for it, why should anyone else?

Still, I longed to swat those mean-spirited hands off me; just one good swipe would do it, but I didn't dare. Back then, the codes of behaviour for kids out with their parents in public were very clear: you did as you were told and the grown-ups were always in the right. And this was even more the case if you were a lone Black foster child like me. My job was to be grateful; grateful that I had been saved from institutional care by a decent, hard-working family; grateful to have a good home. So I didn't protest or duck out of reach the way I longed to; instead I endured these public assaults with an air of private martyrdom. I stood quietly docile, letting myself be handled like something on a plinth at Crufts.

It was this kind of morbid curiosity and derision that led to years of me feeling ashamed and apologetic about my problematic hair.

But if I was destined to a lifetime of bad hair, I'd spotted a cinema poster that gave me a wild kind of hope. As a career pathway, it might just be the future answer to my prayers.

Audrey Hepburn looked so beautiful and serene in *The Nun's Story* that I began to fancy myself looking quietly sensational in a nun's habit. And why not? I was religious enough, wasn't I? I rarely missed Sunday school, I loved singing hymns and I said my prayers every night: 'Matthew, Mark, Luke and John, bless the bed that I lie on.' What's more, I was enthralled by the Bible stories and I positively relished some of the language: 'And when she saw him, she was troubled at his saying and cast in her mind what manner of salutation this should be.' Words like these had a powerful hold over my imagination, and I could easily see myself swathed in black, murmuring prayers in a dimly lit chapel. Maybe I'd even become a missionary and do some good in the world. But best of all, in one of those fetching white wimples, I'd look as cute and pious as Audrey, and I would never have to worry about my hair again. The wimple came as part of the job. It commanded respect and reverence and it was a perfect cover-up for unsightly hair. Yes, the idea of sliding about devoutly, fondling a rosary, had a real romantic appeal. And from what I could tell, the only entry requirement was that I must be prepared to give my life to God. I couldn't see any problem with that. At seven years old, it honestly didn't seem like such a tall order.

# CHAPTER THREE

# ROYAL DUTY

'Give me my robe, put on my crown;
I have immortal longings in me'
ANTONY AND CLEOPATRA, SHAKESPEARE

'Who me? *Again?*'

I fake surprise then slump my shoulders, resigned, before the teacher cuts me a warning glance and hands me my costume for the school play.

I'm nine years old and it's that time of year again. The school Nativity play looms large and I'm required to reprise my role as 'one of the Three Kings' for the third year running. Whether I'm to be Balthazar, Melchior or Caspar is never made clear because nobody seems to know, much less care. What we do know is that as the only Black kid in the class, there is only one role for me in the Nativity play. It goes without saying that I will play one of the kings. What else? My colour adds a touch of exotic authenticity; it gingers things up around the familiar set piece of the crib. Personally, I would like to know exactly *which* king I'm meant to be. You see it makes a difference, because I'd much rather be bearing the gift of gold or frankincense than offering baby Jesus the 'bitter perfume' of myrrh, with all that 'sorrowing, sighing, bleeding, dying' stuff predicted in the Christmas carol. It doesn't help that when I ask for some clarification, the teacher gives me a weary smile, 'You choose. You can be whichever one you like.'

Apparently, one is as good as the other. So I settle on Melchior, Bringer of Gold, because although I love the sound of the word 'frankincense', I'm still not entirely sure what it is and it seems to me that you can't go wrong with gold. But I also like the idea of calling myself 'King Mel', which feels like the name of a real-life character with a bit of personality. I'm just quibbling, of course, because whatever I call myself, nothing alters the fact that for all their stately fanfare, the Three Kings are no fun and everyone knows it. They show up late to the party like a trio of Gloomy Gusses, plodding solemnly on stage to that death march 'We Three Kings'. Talk about killing the mood.

The teacher's reproving look isn't lost on me as I take my costume, but I won't pretend that I'm not disappointed. Last year, I'd begged to be an angel. I'd had it with the dreary kings. I wanted to be a joyous part of the Nativity. I wanted to flutter and flit about the stage bringing 'tidings of great joy', not drag on at the end like part of a funeral cortège. Best of all, as one of the heavenly hosts, I would get to strap on a pair of wings and wear one of those fabulous silver halos attached to a hairband that bobbed and shimmered under the stage lights. But my request to play a lighter, more fun role in the Nativity had been denied.

'Oh, *do* be sensible, Tina,' the teacher had said, shaking her head impatiently as if she'd never heard anything so ridiculous.

So this year, after that warning glare, I know better than to make a fuss; I'm sensible. I'm resigned. Why put up a fight? Being typecast isn't so bad, I suppose. After all, some of the other kids don't have any real part in the play at all. They simply shuffle on stage in old dressing gowns with a teacloth tied to their heads with one of their dad's ties. Behold, the people of Bethlehem: the locals. So look on the bright side, I tell myself. Through no special talent of my own other than looking usefully 'dark and foreign', I've bagged myself a major role. I ought to be thankful. At least I'm not the back end of the donkey.

Now, I inspect the bundle in my lap without enthusiasm. It's the standard-issue kingly raiment. One green velvet curtain, one battered tea caddy and one gold cardboard crown covered in 'gems' of coloured paper. I've grown a lot since last year, so my curtain-cum-cloak will be halfway up my legs this time round, and I already hate that stupid crown. Where is it written that a king must wear a crown? Hadn't I seen a painting of the Nativity in a book where the Three Kings all wore magnificent jewelled and feathered turbans? Fantastic headgear that looked so stylish and cool. What would it take? A length of old cloth and a borrowed brooch and I bet I would look as royal as the best of them. In fact, it's exactly the sort of style that King Mel, who I've decided is the upbeat one of the three, would go in for. It's far more exotic than any crummy cardboard crown.

I toy with the idea of 'accidently' trampling or sitting on my crown, squashing it out of all recognition. *Honestly, Miss, I didn't see it. I didn't even know it was there.* If I had my way, I'd like to toss it straight in the bin. But it wouldn't be any use if I did. They'd soon make a replacement. In fact, I'd probably have to make it myself.

*Why don't they get it?* I wonder. The thing won't fit. That flimsy cardboard is no match for the springy texture of my hair. It doesn't stand a chance. Without a dozen sturdy hair grips anchoring it to my scalp, it will pop off my head like a cork. I had only to think of last year, when it had taken two determined teachers to wrestle it into place. With my head bowed, I couldn't see their faces, but I could hear the gasps of frustration and feel the tempers fraying as my hair stubbornly resisted their efforts and the crown refused to stay put.

'Your hair just *will not* cooperate!' one of them cried, as I felt another hairpin stab into my scalp.

Who was she telling? My uncooperative hair was my private shame. The trouble was that it was quickly becoming public. The sight of two teachers trying to battle my hair into submission was too good a spectacle to miss; soon a growing crowd formed around us – the shepherds, the angels, the ox and the random sheep all gathered to giggle and gawp. My hair was putting up one hell of a fight and as if to compensate for the trouble it was causing, I stood as still as a statue and, now that I had an audience, tried not to whimper or wince.

The teachers were not to be bested by a mop of tight, unruly hair. Finally, they stood back in triumph.

'There you are! That crown's not going anywhere now, so don't you worry.'

I smiled weakly. I wasn't worried, just glad that they had stopped. The crown wouldn't budge because they had pinned it so tightly that my hair hurt and my eyes watered. By the time the audience had joined the cast singing 'O Come, All Ye Faithful', I'd got a tension headache and I couldn't wait to rip the thing off my head.

This time I didn't want any of the teachers making a drama of it with all of their huffing and puffing, so I quietly disappeared into the girls' toilets where I began a private tug of war. I didn't even care that when I finally wrenched the thing off my head, along with it came clumps of my own hair. Days later, I was still finding hair pins bent like paperclips buried in the thick tangle of my roots.

Yes, a turban was the perfect solution for all concerned; a lot less trouble for the teachers and a lot less painful for me. Perhaps I would dare to suggest it. I would look just as stately as the others and nobody, least of all myself, would have to worry about my hair. It would be a case of out of sight, out of mind.

It was all right for the other two kings. They were always boys and their hair didn't fight back. They had short, normal hair that needed just a couple of hair grips to keep their crowns in place. Their hair behaved. It didn't have to be flattened and tugged and restrained with industrial-strength grips. It didn't try the patience of the teachers. And that's another thing. Three *Kings*. In case no one had noticed, *I was a girl*. So why was I lumped in with the boys? Why was I always playing a boy's part?

So here we go again. We are lining up in the wings getting ready to 'follow yonder star'. The angels are already on stage proclaiming 'peace on earth goodwill to all men' to the shepherds, who, in my opinion, are doing a poor job of being 'sore afraid'; one of them is actually waving to his mum in the audience. As usual, all the angels are girls, and back here, still in the shadows and waiting for our big entrance, I eye them with undisguised envy. I can't help thinking how one of those lovely halos would have nestled nicely even in my rebellious hair. Who knows, I might even have looked pretty given half a chance.

# CHAPTER FOUR

# FROM THE BROTHERS GRIMM TO SILVIKRIN

Like a lot of kids, I used to hate having my hair washed at bath time. It wasn't about the hair any more, it was about the water; lashings of it being thrown over my head and pouring down my face again and again. The sensation panicked me into a kind of wild hysteria. With eyes blinded and smarting from shampoo, I gulped down mouthfuls of soapy water. I choked, I spluttered, I thrashed and splashed. The water flooding my face made me feel as if I couldn't breathe. In my child's mind, I couldn't work out why, oh why, were they trying to drown me?

Years later with my own small daughter, I spared her the same shampoo meltdown that I'd suffered, by investing in a shampoo shield. This was a stiff rubber disc with a hole in the middle allowing me to draw her hair through the hole and wash it while letting the water and shampoo splash onto the disc and well away from her face. Shampoo-time became a joy. She looked like a little flower in the shampoo shield. With eyes wide open, she laughed and played with the spray of water splattering around her. It was like sitting under an umbrella during a rainstorm.

But for me as a kid, it was only when I began taking swimming lessons at the local pool that I finally overcame the fear of water all over my face; until then, shampoo-night was a fraught and dismal business.

Still, it was OK. It was all fine, because after all that bathtime stress, there were soothing bedtime stories to look forward to. There was *The Tinderbox* and *The Emperor's New Clothes* and *The Snow Queen*. And there were the intriguing names of Rip Van Winkle, Rumpelstiltskin and then, of course, there was the problematic Rapunzel.

'Rapunzel, Rapunzel! Let down your hair! So that I may climb thy golden stair.'

I won't pretend: Rapunzel may have fascinated me, but I couldn't warm to her, at least not at first. No-uh. For us girls whose hair *did not move*, this chick with the never-ending tresses that doubled as a rope ladder was like a bad joke.

I know, I know; the poor gal had been kidnapped by the wicked witch who was holding her prisoner in the tower. She was the classic damsel in distress. Yet I struggled to sympathise with her plight as my envy for her hair outweighed my compassion for the fix she was in. Rapunzel had that 'must-have' characteristic of every fairy-tale princess I'd ever seen in every storybook – the one thing that every man, be he prince or pauper, desired and prized in his true love – Rapunzel had long, lustrous hair and she had it by the yard.

Like every little girl, I gasped with shock when, having discovered Rapunzel's hair-ladder antics with the prince, the vengeful witch lopped off her wondrous tresses and banished Rapunzel to wander for ever in the deserts of time. That was going too far. And yet at the same time, this, I could relate to; this was something I understood. I knew what it meant to feel punished for your hair, to feel alienated because of it. Maybe Rapunzel and I had more in common than I had at first imagined. Didn't my own childhood fantasies of becoming a nun have something of the same sense of martyrdom, resignation and isolation? Yeah, I know how *that* feels, I thought, finally empathising with the castaway heroine.

So the story of Rapunzel is all about hair as man-bait. Sure, there's a lot more to the story – jealousy, betrayal, revenge blah blah – but who really remembers any of that stuff? The enduring image is of that hot babe marooned in the tower, shaking free her cascade of golden hair for the prince to shimmy up, like a monkey up a rope. Rapunzel is a beauty all right, but without the hair, there's no story. Her hair *is* the story.

I'm pretty sure that any kid will tell you that the message in Rapunzel is clearer than skywriting: long, lustrous (and preferably blonde) hair is the female passport to love and happiness. And the longer, the blonder and the more bountiful, the better. Even Disney saw the dollar signs in this message when it brought out its very own singing and dancing 3D computer-animated version of Rapunzel in 2010, *Tangled*, apparently renaming the story from *Rapunzel* to give it some boy-appeal. (Ker-ching!) *Tangled* was one of the highest-grossing films of that year.

It's not news. Success in the shape of a long, shining mane of hair is a message that's as true today as it ever was. Men desire it and women want it. 'Twas ever thus. Check the billboards, TV ads and the glossy magazines: it's an idea that has a powerful hold on us. From the Brothers Grimm to Silvikrin, a girl doesn't need much in this life, but it *really* helps if she's got the *right kind* of hair.

What's more, she had better be able to work it. She'd better learn how to flick it and swing it and toss it and twirl it around her fingers thoughtfully or suggestively. As a kid, I saw that *moving hair* had a whole language that I was destined never to learn. There were gestures and signals and idle fidgeting behaviours that would never be part of my physical vocabulary.

So where did that leave us kinky-haired girls whose hair

refused to give an inch, let alone flow half a mile down the side of a tower and pull us a prince?

Where were we in the storybooks? I never saw us or anyone who looked remotely like us. Apart from being a little too on the dusky side for a princess, we lacked the essential hair allure. Apparently our tight, wiry curls had no 'comehitherness' in the world of fairy tales. But just imagine if the prince had looked up to the tower and seen a lovely girl with silky brown skin and a stupendous dark halo of natural hair, and that her hair was crackling with its own energy and magic.

'Rapunzel, Rapunzel, are you still up there? Come on, girl, comb out your 'fro.'

Here's a Rapunzel story I'd love to read. A Rapunzel story with a new twist. She may not be able to let her hair down, but, oh boy, she can let it out! Unlike the original Rapunzel, Afro-Rapunzel's hair defies gravity. It's got spring, it's got bounce, it holds secrets. It has its *own* language and is full of its *own* untold stories.

So hey, Rapunzel. Get in synch with your kink, baby!

And if that sounds like a throwback to the '60s and '70s, well that's exactly what it is – because that's when our natural kinky hair, in the shape of the dramatic 'Afro', came into its own.

## CHAPTER FIVE

# FEELING GROOVY, BABY

Whether you were around then or whether you're just hearing it for the first time, you have to know that the '60s and '70s were the golden age of natural Black hair. This was a time when fashion *and* politics conspired to make the Afro not just acceptable but *desirable*. That's when we started hearing phrases like 'Black is beautiful' and 'Say it loud, I'm Black and I'm proud'. As usual, here in Britain we were late to the party, but eventually we were forced to take our cue from America.

In 1968, *Hair: The American Tribal Love-Rock Musical* took London by storm. With its hippy culture, nudity, profanity and anti-war sentiment, it was controversial all right, but it nevertheless captured the restless spirit of the times. It was *Hair* that adopted the Afro into what became an iconic publicity image that was seen worldwide; an image that became synonymous with the peace-seeking hippy generation of 'Make love not war, *man*'.

And suddenly, the Afro was everywhere you looked. It was the last word in style in international fashion spreads such as *Vogue* and *Vanity Fair*. Black models were out there rocking their Afros, celebrating the extraordinary beauty of themselves and their natural hair. These girls with their dark, springy curls looked as chic and sophisticated as any of the sleek-haired models that came before them.

In the world of Black entertainment, any artist who was 'hip to their own trip' or 'where it's at' was sporting an Afro. In fact, it was almost compulsory to your credibility in the music business. Aretha Franklin, Diana Ross, the Jackson Five, the Temptations, the Four Tops were all 'keeping it real' with a carefully groomed 'fro. But perhaps it was with the hard-hitting action movie *Shaft*, and its iconic score by Isaac Hayes, that the Afro actually found its own funky groove. As the slick, tough and hyper-sexed vigilante, PI Shaft was single-handedly cleaning up the streets of Harlem and he was doing it in style. Clad in leather and wearing a sleekly trimmed Afro, Shaft, the man, personified the jittery rhythms of that famous theme tune.

It seemed as if Black people's natural hair had suddenly got emancipated. In the Black civil rights movement across America, the Afro became a political badge of honour. It was seen as a way of reclaiming an identity that had been devalued in white culture. Across Black communities in America, men wore their Afro combs or 'picks' jammed into their hair like a tribal adornment. Their Afro was a matter of pride. The Afro comb was not just a political emblem but a sign of collective identity. And now that the Afro was so hip and groovy, well, guess what? Now everybody wanted an Afro – men and women, Black *and* white. White people who had secretly been ashamed of their big hair now let it grow out, happily combing it out to mimic the fashionable Afro.

I was still in school when those first stunning images of beautiful Black women wearing their Afros like dark, fluffy halos started to appear in the fashion magazines. They looked sensational. Their hair was their whole look. Finally. Here was a look for my kind of hair and it was *so hot it was cool.* All at once, my kind of hair was the hair to have. It was all part of a new buzz of excitement around *just being Black* and I longed to be part of it. The first time I heard Bob and Marcia's song 'Young, Gifted and Black' on the radio, I felt a new sense of identity and pride. The lyrics were loaded with such promise and optimism.

This was powerful stuff to someone like me. As a Black face whose only experience of life was in a white space, the song felt like a joyful affirmation. It was a seal of approval for my uniqueness. It was good to know that somewhere out there a celebration was going on about looking the way I did and having this kind of hair. But the truth is I was a long way away from that excited buzz where I lived. I didn't have the nerve to grow out an Afro.

The way I saw it? If you were a fashion model or maybe singing on the Tamla Motown label, well then, OK, you could definitely pull off an Afro. And if you were a Black American political activist like Angela Davis, well again, 'right on, soul sista'. It was OK for them. There were others around like them; others who appreciated your style and recognised what it meant. But for a lone Black teenager like me, trapped in the hinterlands of North Yorkshire, a real Afro was too much of a statement. I didn't have the confidence to carry it off in isolation. And why would I draw any more attention to my Black self than I already had? No. Forget the Afro. I was working the 'nofro' look. By the time I was fourteen, I was playing my hair *down* not *up*. I was trying to work my unorthodox hair into the mainstream.

I remember spending hours teasing out the tough kinks in my hair with a big wide-toothed comb until my scalp prickled with pain. While still damp, I parted my hair into small sections and slathered each one with sticky globs of setting gel. Next, I wound the gluey strands around big plastic rollers; these were of the hard and spiky variety, and the whole operation felt like wrestling with small hedgehogs. Then I skewered the rollers to my scalp with little plastic spears like a pincushion. Left in overnight, the rollers temporarily tamed the tough kinks in my hair into a looser wave I could work with. While the whole operation didn't straighten my hair, it did make it appear *straighter*. I spent so many nights sleeping on that prickly pillow like a saint in a hair shirt. But a sore scalp and a headache seemed a small price to pay for looking (or so I believed) less *ethnic*. It's a word I've never got on with; like *sputnik* and *beatnik*, in my mind, it's a word that suggests something weirdly off-beat, and this wasn't a look I was going for.

I seem to remember that I was mad at my hair all through my teens. I couldn't find a good word to say about it. I hated its toughness and its wiriness. I believed that it was holding me back from ever looking as attractive or as fashionable as all my white friends. Sure, I could wear the mini-skirts and the bell-bottom trousers, I definitely had the figure for them, but with my gravity-defying hair, I couldn't pull off the same look as them. With their neat bunches, ponytails and plaits, their hair had all the bounce and swing of the '60s dolly girls we saw in the teen magazines. With no guidelines for hair like mine, I battled on privately, stretching it straighter with rollers or dampening it so that I could pat its bulk down into a more even shape.

# CHAPTER SIX

# FURTHER EDUCATION

While the rest of my schoolmates were all headed to university, my predicted grades weren't impressive enough to tempt any offers onto a degree course. I had only myself to blame: I loved the camaraderie of school life more than the focused study that ensured good results. Exams came and went, the end of sixth form loomed and I realised that my membership to the only social club I knew was about to expire. I'd fitted in at school. I'd made damn sure of it. At first, I was active in sports; I was in the hockey team in winter and the athletics team in summer. I liked winning, but I lacked the bullish drive to keep on winning the way that was expected once the teachers had sniffed out your promise. What's more, I didn't care for the regimen of training and practise that came along with being on the team. All those shrill whistles and barked instructions from zealous PE teachers soon sapped my enthusiasm for the school's sporting life altogether. Instead, without knowing it, I was developing a reputation for being a 'bit of a character' or what I later heard Americans refer to as a 'smartass'. I might not be one of the cleverest in the class, but I was always quick off the draw with the glib one-liners and the witty repartee. It became a kind of game, where friends would feed me material just to see how fast I could punt it back with a comic edge to it. The art of not taking life seriously seemed to come naturally to me. Of course, none of this made me a favourite in the staff room, but I had a solid group of pals who liked my style enough to stick with me through all seven years of grammar school. I found that being popular in my gang was much more satisfying than trying to impress the teachers and this was reflected in my breezy approach to my studies. But now it was all coming to an end. Now I was destined to watch my friends scatter to universities across the country where they would go on to flourish and form new friendships. They were all moving on and I was about to get left behind and forgotten. As my friends anticipated student life, it was hard to share the buzz of excitement as they traded information on freshers' week, halls of residence and reading lists. I had nothing to contribute. They were already speaking a different language. The gap between us was already widening. And while no one actually voiced it, I could tell from their slippery glances that some of them were feeling sorry for me. It was such a shame. Unlike them, I hadn't managed to secure a university place. What was that smell? Was that the faint whiff of failure that I was giving off?

I could have enrolled in a local college for a year to resit my exams and play catch-up or maybe signed up for a secretarial course; but these seemed like lame options compared to the rolling success of my friends. At the same time, I knew I wasn't ready for the rigours of the working world. All I'd ever done was a little weekend waitressing and babysitting stints for a family with three school-age kids. What was I good for? Everyone else was striding confidently into their future, but what would become of me? I had no calling and no direction. I would end up drifting into the first job that came along. The thought of myself as a dogsbody being batted between departments in some dreary office was enough to help my brain fog to clear.

I was quick-witted, resourceful and had an independent spirit that yearned to travel. I decided that I quite liked the idea of myself as an au pair; an au pair in Italy sounded even better. 'Oh, Tina?' I could hear them say. 'Didn't you know? She's living in Italy now.' It had a devil-may-care ring that appealed to both the romantic and the rebel in me. With a little imagination and daring, I might still turn academic failure into personal triumph. My further education would be to take off on a foreign adventure;

and unlike all my friends, there was only one book on my required reading list and that was *Teach Yourself Italian*.

Italy was different back then. Communism – or at least the bourgeois version of communism that no Russian queuing in a bread line would have recognised – was one of the few 'isms' that you heard a lot about in '70s Italy. These were the years when the Italian Communist Party (PCI) with its socialist manifesto played a major role in the political scene of the day and was taking on the old guard of the right. But as for feminism, sexism and racism, if they had heard of them at all, these were still foreign concepts to most Italians.

Unlike in the UK and France, Italy's Black population is a fairly recent one that has only developed over the past thirty years. Today, the mass African migration to its southern shores causes social and political tensions for both the migrants and the existing Black population in the country. But rewind to the '70s and Black people were a rare sight in Italy and were likely to meet with curious interest from the Italians.

Black people were something Italians only ever saw on TV and they came in two versions: they were either glamorous entertainers gyrating in sequins or they were the poor, emaciated devils you saw on the news in some forgotten, dust-blown corner of Africa. So a real, live Black girl going about her everyday business on the streets of

Florence was a sight to behold. I was a sensational beast that required close inspection and the Italians stared at me with a bare-faced curiosity that was truly unnerving. They stared as if they had paid good money and I was the entertainment. Sometimes the scrutiny was so intense that I fancied I could hear a David Attenborough-like voice-over in my head, the tone even and reassuring: 'And here we have a rare glimpse of the wiry-haired Black girl, whose distinctive colouring and hair texture make this species so interesting...'

Worst of all was the relentless male attention that quickly went from being a shocking novelty to a blasted nuisance. Men were underfoot wherever I went. They blocked my path or brushed up against me on the narrow pavements or they tried to fall in step with me as I walked. And then there were the kerb-crawlers who cruised by me like tourists at a safari park, murmuring obscenities and offering me a ride as traffic backed up behind them. To someone who'd never had to handle more than a British wolf-whistle (and that only rarely), I couldn't believe that this full-on assault and the lascivious comments were all going on in public and that nobody, except me, seemed to mind. I was horrified to learn that my hi-vis skin colour was an added stimulus to the hyperactive libido of most Italian men – that in their minds, a Black woman was synonymous with sexual availability. I hated being sexualised on sight, but there was little I could do about what I soon realised was considered normal behaviour for Italian men. When I confided to the Italian family I was living with that I found the men intimidating, they shrugged as if they thought I was playing dumb. What did I expect? I was young, female, foreign and, if that wasn't enough, I was Black. I was prime catnip to the Italians. The only advice from my Italian family: better get used to it.

'*Come mai non hai i capelli veri?*' asked Barbara, the precocious four-year-old I was looking after, as I was putting her to bed one night. *Why don't you have real hair?* It seemed a fair question for an Italian kid at the time; a question I might have tried to answer had she not grabbed a handful of my hair as I leaned over to tuck her in and yanked it so viscously that she pulled a handful out at the roots. I howled with pain and instinctively my hand twitched to clout her. But somehow my head overruled my instinct. Instead, I quickly switched off the light and hissed balefully into the dark, '*Buona notte*, Barbara.'

Even at eighteen, I knew I wasn't cut out to be an au pair. I didn't much care for children and I hated any kind of housework, however 'light'. But in the '70s, au pairing for young British girls was the easiest way of getting and staying abroad for a while. Like the gap year, it was the foreign experience that would broaden your horizons and with any luck you might even learn a language. Trapped in the affluent suburbs with my Italian family, I was keen to discover Florence, but just the thought of having to navigate men like an obstacle course was disheartening. On the other hand, I needed to escape the fiendish tot and her doting parents, so on my days off, I forced myself to leave the safety of the apartment and brave the bus into Florence alone.

Once out on the city streets, I knew I had to pick up the pace. To avoid being waylaid, propositioned or pursued by random men, I learned to walk with the brisk, purposeful stride of someone late for an appointment. But it didn't always deter the hard-core pests and sometimes I'd take refuge by diving into a bar where I was forced to order an espresso that I really didn't want. While I was always drawn to its alluring smell as it filtered out into the streets, I couldn't get used to the actual taste of the tiny shots of bitter, syrupy coffee. Meanwhile, I'd learned early in Italy never to look a man in the eye unless he was standing behind a counter serving me, and even then only fleeting-ly, but that didn't stop me overhearing the comments from bystanders around me.

'It's the sun over there in Africa. It does that to their hair. Fries it up tight like that. We saw it when we were out in Ethiopia during the war,' I heard one old campaigner explaining my hair to his mate as they studied me with anthropological interest while I paid for my coffee.

This idea about Afro hair seemed to be a recurring motif in the imagination of Italians back then, as I found out later when I had ditched au pairing to work in a busy tourist shop in the centre of Florence.

I had finally got up the nerve to ask the boss if he would pay me for all the crazy overtime I was doing and in line with my Italian colleagues. The boss was a big Neapolitan built like a brick wall; his slab of a face set in a permanent leer. No matter what time of day, he usually had a glass of whisky clutched in one meaty fist and it was a case of catching him early enough to get any sense out of him at all. When I pitched my case, the boss licked his livery lips and gave me his trademark boozy leer. He liked a laugh as much as the next man and these foreigners he hired over the summer were always good for a chuckle. But when he saw I wasn't joking and that I was expecting some kind of verbal response, he shook his head as if he was undecided whether to be annoyed or amused at my impudence. Not only did I have the nerve to be Black but I was cocky with it. Taking a slug of his whisky, he studied me for a few moments as if trying to guess my weight. Then his leer morphed into a sneer.

'Listen, sweetheart, I don't know where the hell you come from, but wherever it is, the sun must have cooked your brain as well as your hair.'

I took this to be a hard 'no' and returned to the shop

floor quietly fuming. I told myself that I'd asked for the abuse by putting myself in the firing line and that I would have to take it on the chin or start looking for another job. What rattled me more than the flat refusal was that he'd seen my British passport and he knew perfectly well that I was born in England. That's why he'd hired me. My job was to wheedle more dollars out of the American tourists in their own language.

'Just feel these gloves... I know! The leather's like silk, isn't it? Why not get another pair as a gift for someone back home?'

'Told you,' said the other English girl who worked in the shop when I reported my failed bid for equal pay.

That's right, she had told me it would be a useless exercise, and by then I'd been in Italy long enough not to be surprised by the knee-jerk racism, but it still came with a nasty sting. I couldn't bring myself to repeat to her exactly how the boss had turned me down and how I'd lacked both the guts and the ready Italian to protest.

I couldn't speak for the African sun, but it wasn't too long before the Italian sun definitely began to give me some trouble. After the damp climes of northern England, the unrelenting Mediterranean heat was playing havoc with my hair. Perpetually sun-frazzled and dry as straw, it was crying out for some serious moisturising and the frizzy ends needed trimming. Once again, there was no one around with hair like mine to advise me. Maybe it was time to try a professional? I needed help, and desperation must have made me reckless. Steeling every nerve, I walked into an Italian hair salon.

Inside, I'm hit by the convivial buzz of chat and laughter competing with the roar of blow dryers. It's busy and noisy, but my entrance quickly puts a stop to all that. As I walk in, it's as if the whole place freezes and business comes to a standstill. I'm reminded of the moment the mean-eyed cowboy swaggers into the saloon fingering his six-shooter. That's right, folks. There's a stranger in town. Blow dryers snap silent, scissors hover midair like birds of prey and the hubbub of voices trails off into startled whispers. In the movies, this would be the cue for the old barkeep to plead nervously: 'Now see here, mister. We don't want no trouble round here.'

I was no troublemaker, just a Black gal looking for a hair rescue remedy, but to judge from the collective gasp of stylists and clients alike, I might as well have been Medusa, with a head full of hissing serpents dropping in for a shampoo and set. I saw my image multiplied in half a dozen mirrors and it was as if the whole salon was holding its breath.

Suddenly, all eyes swivel in the direction of Rodolfo, the master stylist. A true '70s man, Rodolfo is sporting a fashionable handlebar moustache with sideburns and a shaggy mane of dark shoulder-length hair. In keeping with the times, he's dressed like a glam-rock star in tight hipster flares and his pink shirt gapes open, revealing a gold cross nestling in a thick undergrowth of chest hair.

Rodolfo had been giving the final tweaks to a client as I came in and he had frozen along with the rest of the salon when he first saw me, but now he quickly regains his composure. He steps away from his client and with stagey emphasis he asks what *he* can do for *me* today. This is quite a show and I can feel the whole salon leaning in to hear me state my business. I've reached a point where I can get by in Italian pretty well, but for moments like this, I always rehearse my lines carefully. Only I'd imagined a confidential one-to-one with the stylist. I hadn't bargained on a captive audience and my words come out in a squeaking and apologetic stammer.

'I'd just like... I'd like... just a treatment... *per favore...* a moisturising treatment, I mean. And a trim... yes... a light trim.'

Rodolfo glances at my hair and for a moment I see a look of panic flash across his face, but then with all the dignity of man who knows his limits and isn't afraid to admit them, he says loftily, '*Preferirei di non provare, Signorina.*'

He would rather not attempt it; simple as that. And with a toss of his lustrous locks, Rodolfo turns back to fuss over his client, a petite blonde whose hair he has just lacquered into a stiff helmet.

The salon sprang back to life, although the other stylists were still shaking their heads as they cranked up the blow dryers again and resumed combing and snipping. Their clients exchanged knowing glances with them in the mirrors. Really! Walking in bold as brass with *that hair*! Poor Rodolfo. The man's an accomplished stylist, no doubt about it, but he's not a miracle worker. You couldn't blame him. You had to draw the line.

Rodolfo would rather not, and a dignified retreat seemed the only option. But for a few long moments, I stood frozen with embarrassment before quietly leaving the salon. *Tolgo il disturbo*, as the Italians say politely when they feel they are in the way or troubling someone. Literally it means 'I'll remove the disturbance or trouble (that I'm causing)'.

I felt as if I'd let myself down. Just like with the boss in the tourist shop, in walking into Rodolfo's, I'd set up a scene for my own humiliation. I was asking for it and I blamed myself. What stayed with me was that bolt of panic that shot across Rodolfo's horrified face when he first glanced at my hair. What, *him*? Do something with *that*? It was as if I'd asked him to perform some unnatural act.

It was a good thing that Linda, my flatmate and an art

history student, liked a challenge. A big, blonde athletic girl from Seattle, it was she who came to the rescue of my hair. 'Hell, how hard can this be!' she said as she began tugging at the kinky coils of my hair and snipping the ragged edges. As with most things, when it came to my hair, Linda was fearless. She became my live-in stylist, cutting my hair into a neat crop and smothering it with coconut oil to keep it soft. Much better for the Italian climate, I told myself. But I couldn't help feeling it was a last resort, a crisis crop, and my hair was being 'fettled' again just like the old days as a kid.

The small kitchen of our second-floor flat became our makeshift salon where Linda, humming along to her Carly Simon tape, snipped my hair while I looked out over the glorious, ramshackle roofscape of Florence. Medieval towers and domes and palaces; each stone steeped in a history that had shaped the thinking of the modern world. So how, I wondered, had a nation that had forged the Renaissance with such ingenuity and imagination five hundred years ago, been completely stumped by my kinky hair in 1974?

'Wish I had hair like this. It's got so much character. I'd do all kinds of crazy stuff with it if it were mine. And best of all it stays put.'

I smiled. Linda was being kind. You either had good hair or bad hair like mine, but hair with character? And with all the 'swishability' and sex appeal of her own long, blonde tresses, she couldn't seriously envy my hopeless head of stiff, wiry curls. But I was just glad there was someone around who looked on my hair with a benevolent eye and was prepared to help me manage it. The experience in Rodolfo's salon had shaken my confidence to the core, but now, thanks to Linda, I could begin to see myself in a more kindly light.

# CHAPTER SEVEN

# RENAISSANCE HAIR

There was nothing I could do about the routine racism and, once I learned to ignore the pestering men, there was a lot to love about being in Italy in the '70s. In Florence, there was almost too much to soak up and savour at once. Right on my doorstep, I had sublime, world-class art, and there was fabulous food in the small, lively *trattoria*, hidden in side streets where the tourists rarely ventured. Beauty and style ran through the city like an unbroken thread and every building and piazza pulsed with a history you could feel and breathe. As I got to know the city, it was as if I was getting to know myself better too. I was learning how to survive without the familiar props of place, language and habit. Within a small group of international friends, I shared a dizzy sense of having stumbled upon an earthly paradise, a playground of pleasure and plenty. It was a place where, despite some old-world attitudes, and despite my self-doubts, I might even fall in love.

His name was Marco, and we used to rattle around Florence together in his nifty, little Fiat 500, or what the Italians called a '*cinquecento*'. Back then, it seemed as if every second car on the street in Italy was a spluttering, rumbling *cinquecento*, a tiny toy-like car that what it lacked in size, it made up for in noise. These cars might look like something Mickey Mouse would drive, but they were ideally suited for careering around the narrow streets of Italian towns and you could park them on a sixpence. Shooting across the grand piazzas and roaring along streets no wider than alleys, it was like being driven around in a Dinky toy. While it was true that the confined space inside the car severely restricted movement, these cramped conditions forced an intimacy that made it the ideal car for seduction. In the Fiat *cinquecento*, body contact was inevitable. The slightest change of position, and elbows and thighs were bound to brush. Shift a gear and you couldn't help making a pass. This little car has been the beginning of countless romances in Italy and ours was just one of them.

Besides the thrill of whizzing about Florence in his car, the thing that really blew me away about Marco was that he genuinely loved my hair. Ever since those unfeeling old busybodies had manhandled me as a kid, I've always been wary of people touching my hair. I was nobody's prize poodle, and as I got older, I'd been known to slap away curious hands. But when Marco put his hands in my hair, he did it with a sense of wonder and real pleasure. He loved to draw one of my springy curls out to its full length, laughing with delight when it simply sprang back into place like elastic. To Marco, my hair was a sexy playground and he loved to stroke it and snuffle it like a dog with its favourite bedding. I had always hoped someone might love me despite my hair, but I had never imagined it being a big part of my attraction. When Marco called my hair his '*nido di dolcezza*', or his 'nest of tenderness', I felt as if the whole of me was being loved for the first time. It took me by surprise. I was so used to seeing my hair as the 'enemy' that had to be clobbered into submission. So used to writing it off. Now I would shiver with anticipation when Marco nuzzled at my hair and murmured: '*Che cesto di capelli ricci! Sono così vivi. Sono bellissimi. Quanto mi piacciono questi capelli.*'

*What a basket of curls. They are so alive. So beautiful. I really love this hair.*

Yes. Yes. And yes.

And if that isn't poetry, what is, I should like to know? If *that* doesn't get you learning Italian pretty damn quick, then nothing will. It was as if this man had created a whole new language for my hair that made me feel beautiful and special, a language of praise. I turned his words over in my head like a prayer and I felt transformed. Marco had composed a hymn to my hair. After the dark ages of Rodolfo with his lofty dismissal, I felt as if my hair was having its very own Italian Renaissance, an awakening to its inherent vitality and all its possibilities. Like some medieval troubadour, I was ready to set Marco's words to music. This was where my kinky hair met the fifteenth century in a cultural crossover, where maybe a madrigal accompanied by the simple chords of a lute made perfect sense:

*Che cesto di capelli ricci*
*Vivi e bellissimi*
*Nido di dolcezza*
*Nido di dolcezza*
*Che mi porta via il Cor*

Still buzzing from my Italian adventures, I came back to England and belatedly began a university degree. After two years studying and living in Florence, Italian seemed like the most natural thing to do. And in choosing drama as my subsidiary course, I met Mamie, my Black South African friend, and it was with her help that I began to discover the true versatility of my kind of hair for the first time.

Mamie taught me that the ritual of hair grooming among communities of Black women, wherever they were in the world, was a big part of Black culture. It was a community and a culture I had never known growing up in my white foster home in North Yorkshire, and the more she talked about it, the more I realised that it was an experience that would have given me a very different relationship with my hair from an early age. My hands would have become familiar with its texture; my fingers would have known how to manipulate it.

As a child, Mamie would sit at the knee of her mother or some other female relative or friend known as 'auntie', while they oiled and brushed out her hair before nimbly working it into intricate braids and cornrows. The process often took hours and it was in this intimate company of women that Mamie sat quietly listening to the easy talk and laughter going on over her head. As expert fingers wove her hair, she absorbed the collective wisdom, humour and strength of the women around her, and it had given her a strong sense of her own identity. Care and respect for hair was part of a loving, social ritual that bound Black women in friendship and trust across the generations. The fact that it took time and patience was all part of the natural female bonding process. When I compared this with my own painful and private struggles, I knew that I had missed out on a vital rite of passage towards not just loving my hair but loving my identity.

I may have missed out on the experience, but with Mamie it wasn't too late to get a taste of what that felt like. As Mamie tugged and twisted my hair, we sipped cheap wine, gossiped and swapped our stories, while Joan

Armatrading crooned soulfully in the background. True, there was just the two of us, but it was a relaxing and restorative time with a good friend; a good friend who understood and loved my hair.

'You're lucky that it's so thick,' she said, raking her fingers through its volume in admiration. 'And it's so easy to work with.'

Tell that to Rodolfo back in Florence, I wanted to say. Then I suddenly remembered Linda saying: 'I'd do all kinds of crazy stuff with it if it were mine.'

At the time, I had thought she was just trying to make me feel better. But I wished Linda could see me now, because 'all kinds of crazy stuff' was what Mamie did best. She twisted my hair into complex geometric designs of cornrows close to my scalp, threading pearl beads or fine gold thread into the weave; or she fashioned loose braids that swung and rattled with colourful beads when I moved. And once, when I wanted a special 'look' for a party, she took the loose ends of my braids and looped them together so that they stood upright on the top of my head. It looked amazing. It was as if I had grown my own crown and my hair had become a piece of natural architecture. With this hair not only did I have extra height but my confidence was sky-high too. It was the first time that I'd felt a sense of pride and power in my hair. I remember walking into the party that night feeling like an African Queen.

# CHAPTER EIGHT

# SCANDI-NOIR

'**B**limey, what the hell happened to you? Looks like you've had your head ploughed,' snickered Ron, the boyfriend of one of my housemates, at the bar in the students' union. His two mates obligingly spluttered into their pints. Yeah. Nice one, Ronnie.

In the '70s, you didn't see many Black women in Britain wearing cornrows. In fact, on my small university campus in the north of England, you didn't see many Black women at all. Among the modern foreign language students studying German, French, Spanish, Italian and Scandinavian studies, I was the only non-white student. This meant that bucket-heads like Ron and his mates felt free to say anything they liked to me. Who was to stop them? And anyway, what was my problem? They were just having a laugh.

I was still getting used to the cornrows myself and I

knew that it dramatically altered my look. I'd never had my hair braided close to my head before or my scalp so exposed to the elements. Come to think of it, I'd never seen the natural shape of my head until now. It was still hard to believe that the sheer volume of my hair could be so neatly packed away into these tight, precise rows. Now, between the tension of the braids, I could actually feel fresh air on my head for the first time. Ploughed! You couldn't expect those lager-swilling Neanderthals to appreciate the artistry of it. How could they understand the shared confidence and laughter, the intimacy that had been twisted into each row of these braids? Seeing myself in the mirror, I was reminded of the Italian vineyards, where the ranks of vines follow the soft contours of the hills. What I was wearing on my head was nothing less than my own personal landscape.

For most of the students on the Italian course, the study year abroad couldn't come around soon enough. We'd spent the past two years poring over Italian texts from the medieval to the modern. We had dissected, analysed and critiqued them, and like vultures on a dead carcass, stripped them clean to the bone. We had written ponderous essays about them, regurgitating words such as 'leitmotif' and '*Bildungsroman*' – words guaranteed to warm the frosty hearts of lecturers and tutors alike. Beetling between lectures and the university library, we had written up notes and drafted essay plans, combing the shelves to reference obscure studies on everything from Machiavelli to Calvino. Surely, we had earned some breathing space? Now, as the end of our second year approached, here it was. The study year abroad was clearly in our sights. While we would still have some coursework to complete, the main order of business for the next academic year would be our attachment to high schools in Italy as English language assistants. As *assistenti inglesi*, our job was to help kids in Italian schools get to grips with spoken English, while improving our own fluency in Italian with everyday life experience.

My fellow students were fairly giddy at the prospect of spending nine months in Italy. After all the drills and practise in *conversazioni*, here was their chance to 'go live' with the language; a language that so far, they had only ever test-driven in a controlled environment. They were now about to take it on the road and put it through its paces.

At twenty-three, I was considered a 'mature' student. All of the others had come to university fresh from school and this would be their first experience of living overseas. For most, it would be their very first time abroad without the backup of either family or friends. For them, Italy was the big adventure waiting to happen and they were raring to go. This was the year they would come into their own.

They were eager to dive into all the delights that Italian life would offer, be it food, fashion, football, phenomenal art and whatever romantic opportunities came their way. Just let them at it!

Naturally, I was a little more circumspect than the others about this year. But, then, I told myself, I had every reason to be. By now, I'd spent enough time in Italy to know that, for someone who looked like me, I was probably in for a rough ride in the role of an English language assistant. I was well aware that getting the Italians to accept me as a) English and b) an assistant teacher was asking for a huge leap in their imagination, not to say their belief. That would be my first hurdle before I could expect to get anywhere near a classroom. I told myself I would brazen it out, the way I always did in Italy, but I also knew how mentally exhausting it is when you have to explain and prove yourself *all the time* and to *everyone*. I loved Italy, it was where I felt I had come of age, but like Eve, I had tasted that apple and now I knew too much for my own good.

But before I undertook 'mission impossible' in Italy, eight weeks of the summer lay fallow before me; weeks I was determined not to fritter away in some humdrum job. What I needed was a different experience that would give me a fresh outlook. A summer escapade that would inject

me with a vibrant new energy, leaving me suitably chilled
for whatever the Italians might throw at me.

I had a Finnish friend, Helmi, studying in Helsinki
whose family had a fruit and veg farm in Central Finland.
It was strawberry-picking season, and she invited me to
join her, first in Helsinki, then to travel north together
to work on the family farm. It was a chance to see some
of this unknown country, make a little money and spend
some time together with my friend. Of course I would
go. I'd heard that the natural beauty of Finland was won-
derfully unspoiled and I liked that it was slightly off-grid
from the well-worn European trails. Finland would do
the trick. With its dense forests, clear air and crystal lakes,
it would be like a refreshing shot in the arm. It was the
ideal *aperitivo* that would clear my palette for Italy.

To be precise, it wasn't my first time in Scandinavia, nor
in Helsinki. I'd met Helmi at the end of an Interrail trip
I'd taken to Scandinavia three years before. It was while I
was still living in Florence and sharing a flat with Linda,
my American friend who doubled as my live-in hairstylist.

In all her blue-eyed blondeness, it was no surprise that
Linda traced her heritage back to Norway. Her parents,
back in Seattle, had never seen the old country and had
little curiosity about it, but Linda was dead set on visiting
Norway while she was still studying in Europe. While I

had no real interest in Scandinavia myself, Linda could be very persuasive.

'Jeez, you gotta come. It'll be cheap and real fun. Just think, we can go *anywhere*. Every day we get to decide where we want to be.'

The next thing I knew, she had out her atlas plotting the trains and ferries that would take us through Germany, Denmark and Sweden, then all the way to Oslo and finally Bergen, where Linda planned to do some ancestral digging.

We both knew who we were in Italy: the foreign girls who had learned to confidently handle ourselves and could give as good as we got. But it was as if we'd left those savvy girls behind in Florence. In Scandinavia, we were in unfamiliar territory, not just foreigners but strangely dislocated by both language and surroundings. Now we both felt awkward and uncertain about everything. That September, Florence was still in the grip of a clinging heat, but in Oslo, it was as if we'd entered a world of perpetual dampness. We moved about in the kind of unrelenting downpours that made you wonder if you would ever be dry again. The locals were well equipped. In their heavy-duty waterproofs, they all looked like sea-rescue workers about to launch a lifeboat into raging waters. Only foreigners, like us, battled with their sodden umbrellas, in the same way that in Italy only the tourists wear ridiculous straw hats. We staggered about half-blinded by the rain while the Norwegians slipped around us like supple fish. Occasionally, the rain let up long enough to reveal a watery sun. At these times, there was such a clean, tingling feel to the air that it felt as if the whole world had just brushed its teeth.

With her fresh-faced, all-American blondeness, Linda fit right in among the Scandinavians and she moved about relatively unnoticed. In Oslo, she could easily have passed for another Norwegian, and when I told her so, she grinned, delighted. These, after all, were her people, and although she didn't speak the language, she already felt an ancestral connection with them. But in 1974 as a Black girl in Norway, there was no chance of me merging unnoticed into the general population. Among the Aryan looks of the natives, my dark skin and wiry Afro made me stand out like a black exclamation mark. But I was glad to see that the Norwegians kept it low-key. They looked, but they didn't stop and stare at me like a fairground attraction, the way the Italians did. There was a polite reserve, respect even, about the Norwegians' looks, and they didn't feel compelled to make body contact or trail behind me muttering a lot of nonsense about their liking for 'hot chocolate' or 'dark meat'. As a good-looking American blonde, Linda had got more attention in Italy than she could handle too, and we both appreciated the more relaxed vibe of Scandinavia. It had been the same in Denmark and Sweden, where we had been able to go about our business untroubled by the kind of agitated male attention we had learned to put up with in Italy. It was refreshing and, I realised, liberating, not to be always seen as some kind of a sexual trigger. It reminded us of how much effort we put into being on the defence in Italy, where dodging men had become second nature. Up here, it felt as if we were able to 'stand at ease' and be ourselves. There was nothing wrong with being noticed, as long as people didn't try to encroach.

In Italy, thanks to Linda, I'd learned to protect my hair from the heat with coconut oil and, sometimes, olive oil, but the damp air in Oslo defeated us both. Linda's long, sleek hair was often plastered to her head and she spent a lot of time at the youth hostel wafting her hair under the wall-attached dryer. Meanwhile, my hair simply shrank into tight, knotty coils that resisted even the prongs of my Afro pick. Instead of a neat little Afro, my hair dried out into a shapeless, brittle frizz.

'Here, try this,' said Linda, flipping me a sachet of mayonnaise she'd pocketed from one of the self-service restaurants. 'Then rinse it off in the shower.'

I looked at her dubiously. Really? Cover my hair in salad dressing? More in desperation than belief, I smeared the stuff over my hair and, with Linda's nods of encouragement,

I worked it well into my scalp. To my amazement, this mayonnaise hair rescue worked. The treatment made my hair not only pliable again but it gave it a glossy sheen and the frizz effect had completely gone. I was back in control again. It was OK. I would smell like a tossed salad for a while, but I was back on track with my hair. From then on, we took every opportunity to filch mayonnaise sachets wherever we found them.

One day, we sloshed our way to the Edvard Munch museum to find we practically had the place to ourselves. Used to the winding queues we saw every day outside the Uffizi in Florence, this almost felt like a private viewing. Rain-flattened and with shoes squelching, we clattered around the near-empty rooms gaping at the whey-faced, disconnected figures in the portraits. Maybe it was all the rain and the strange sense of dislocation I'd been feeling in Norway, but entering the world of Edvard Munch suddenly felt dangerously dark. So many of the paintings seemed bereft of any hope and I could feel their mood of melancholy beginning to settle. The pale woman with the long red hair like creeping tendrils was particularly troubling. This woman, with her ghostly pallor and fore-boding attitude, appeared repeatedly among the portraits like a restless phantom. I suddenly felt overwhelmed by the weight of a nameless sadness. I couldn't take it any more. I needed to sit down. I made my way back to a bench at the entrance, where I sat and waited for Linda. Meanwhile, I flicked through one of the free brochures I'd picked up on the way in. Twenty minutes later, Linda slumped down beside me and, like some wounded animal, let out a prolonged groan.

'I know!' I moaned.

To capture our mood of desolation, I read her one of Munch's quotes from the brochure I was looking at: 'The angels of fear, sorrow and death stood by my side from the day I was born.'

We both dropped our chins to our chest and exchanged a doleful glance. Then Linda's shoulders began to shake and soon we were both snorting with a mad, unbridled laughter. Poor old Munch may have been teetering on the edge of insanity, but he wasn't going to take us with him. Not just yet, anyway. We hurried out of the museum giggling like a couple of inmates escaping the asylum.

From Oslo, we took the spectacular cross-country train to Bergen, which flies high over fjords and lakes with stunning mountain vistas. Unable to take our eyes off the ravishing views, we hardly noticed that the journey took seven hours. Bergen was as wet as the rest of Norway, but it was a pretty, neat and tidy city with a lovely harbour and great seafood. Linda had reached her destination in her quest for family connections and in Bergen we parted ways. The night before I left, Linda gave me a postcard of

Munch's most famous painting the, *The Scream*. But she had customised the postcard for me. Around the bald, distorted head of the screaming figure, she had sketched an electrified Afro. *The Afro-Scream in Oslo*, she had written on the back. The postcard is long lost, but this was one of my lasting memories of the trip with Linda.

Alone now, and with another sequence of ferries and trains, I worked my way back to Stockholm, where I wanted to take a closer look at the city. It was in the youth hostel in Stockholm that I met a group of Norwegian students who were on their way to study in Helsinki. Up until that point, Finland had not figured on my personal map, but the Norwegians were a merry bunch and they convinced me that, if nothing else, the overnight ferry would be 'very big fun'. Scandinavia had been interesting so far, and I'd had some laughs with Linda, but, if I'm honest, this last leg hadn't been a lot of fun. It had been exhausting jumping on and off trains and ferries and finding my way around unfamiliar cities to youth hostels, museums and cheap eateries. What's more, the incessant rain had hung over me like a veil of tears. Travelling solo now, I had a strange sense of feeling outside myself and disconnected. I believe it was the first time in my life that I felt lonely. Now the Norwegians were promising 'very big fun' on the ferry and I still had a week before my Interrail card ran out.

The overnight ferry from Stockholm to Helsinki takes about sixteen hours, and the Norwegians were right: it was like being on board a big floating party. At this stage, I still hadn't experienced any of the excesses of student life, and I soon realised that I was way out of my depth with this crowd. The Norwegians, I discovered, don't like to drink; they *love* to drink. Russian vodka seemed to be the preferred tipple and with large quantities of duty-free booze available on board, the party kicked off as soon as we set sail. I later found out that many Finns and Swedes take the ferry at the weekend just for a couple of cheap nights out drinking. Three hours into the voyage and four – or was it five? – vodkas down, I was dry-heaving into a toilet bowl and wishing I was dead. In the next stall I'd caught sight of one of the Norwegian girls in the same condition, her long hair trailing into the bowl where she vomited.

I found myself a quiet corner in the seating area where I could stretch out and quietly moan. I told myself it was the rocking motion of the ferry not the vodka that wasn't agreeing with me. Closing my eyes only made things worse. All I wanted was to get back onto dry land and I didn't care where – Russia would do just as well as Finland. My thoughts drifted back to that poor girl I'd left still hugging the toilet bowl and groaning. Say what you like: one good thing about an Afro like mine is that I would never be in danger of throwing up on it.

I have no memory of getting off the ferry or how we made our way to the campus at Helsinki University, where, by the way, I knew I had absolutely no business. The truth is I had ended up in Finland on a whim and now had nowhere else to go. It didn't seem to bother the Norwegians who had adopted me as an interesting camp-follower, but the Finnish welcoming party were definitely puzzled to see me, loitering among the group of Norwegians. But to my surprise, the Finns treated me like an unexpected VIP guest, an added bonus. Everyone seemed thrilled to speak English with me and they were genuinely intrigued by the mystery of my Black-British-Italian background. It was only now that I discovered that the study of trees, or dendrology (a lovely new word for me), was the reason for the Norwegians' visit. As the most heavily forested country in Europe, Finland is a leader in the field of forestry studies. With 75 per cent of Finland's land mass covered in forests, trees drive its prosperous economy and attract students and researchers on sustainable forestry from around the world.

'You can take the Finn out of the forest, but you can't take the forest out of the Finn,' said Helmi, one of the welcoming Finnish students who generously shared her room on campus with me.

Helmi and I quickly became friends, and while I turned down her invite to a lecture on soil erosion, I was happy to be introduced to the sacred culture of the sauna. Sitting naked together as we both sweated like cheeses was the beginning of a beautiful friendship that lasts to this day. Naturally, all that sauna steam was playing hell with my Afro, but I still had some mayonnaise sachets stowed away in my backpack.

So, yes, I had been to Finland before, but only just, when I had piggybacked on the Norwegians' trip. Back then, it had been no more than a pit stop and I'd seen nothing but the student campus with barely a glimpse of Helsinki. But that's when I had first met Helmi, and we had got on so well that we had continued to stay in touch. Now, three years later, we would have a proper chance to renew our friendship and I had the entire summer before I started working as a language assistant in Italy to discover not only Helsinki but the unknown country that lay beyond.

Central Finland is breathtakingly beautiful. Dotted with thousands of lakes surrounded by pine, spruce and birch forests, everything about it says clean, healthy living and a love of nature and the outdoors. I spent several weeks with Helmi picking strawberries on her family's remote farm while her non-English-speaking parents regarded me with fond bemusement. It was clear they were not quite sure what manner of beast I might be or how exactly their daughter's path had crossed with mine. Still, they were warm and extremely welcoming, and with Helmi as interpreter, her mum tentatively asked me questions. The Black girl, who lives in England where she studies Italian, but who is now here in Finland? It didn't add up and I could see her point. The Finnish language is not remotely related to the other Scandinavian languages, so I rarely had a clue what was being said.

What I did understand was that Helmi's mum was fascinated by my hair. I frequently saw her sneaking glances at it and looking abashed when she saw I noticed. One day, she shyly asked if she might be allowed to just touch it, if I didn't mind. For once, I found that I didn't. I knew it was asked with affectionate curiosity. I had just given it a mayonnaise treatment, following one of the daily sessions in the family sauna, and I could feel the sense of surprise in her fingertips when she realised it was soft and silky to the touch. I let her comb her fingers through it and fondle the texture, thinking once again how different this felt from those interfering, unfeeling hands of the Yorkshire hausfraus from my youth. I wished that she could have seen my hair when Mamie put it in braids. She would have been utterly captivated.

Helmi translated: 'She loves your hair. She wants to have your hair.'

Even Helmi's usually taciturn father laughed at that; like us, no doubt, he was trying to envision this plump, middle-aged, Finnish farmer's wife sporting an Afro.

I soon found that strawberry picking was knee-aching, shoulder-wrenching and back-breaking work and I wasn't used to it. Other than riding my bike, student life made few physical demands on me, and I was wholly unprepared for farm labour. Helmi was a hardy farm-girl at heart, who could easily pick two trays of strawberries as I laboured to fill one. At the end of the day, I would totter back to the farmhouse and drop like a sandbag onto the bed. Everything hurt. On the bright side, the strawberry wine that Helmi's mum brewed was like a wonder drug for aches and pains. After two glasses, you felt nothing at all, except a tremendously warm sense of well-being.

Finland is full of so many lakes; everywhere, the sunlight bounces off sparkling stretches of water hemmed by dark pine forests. Helmi's family had their very own lake at the bottom of the garden, where they kept a small rowboat anchored. In summer, it's still broad daylight at midnight in Finland, and one night Helmi rowed me out into the lake and into a vast world of blue-green silence. Maybe it was the strawberry wine, but like Ratty and Mole on the river in *The Wind in the Willows*, between the whispering leaves of the birches and the rhythmic slap of the oars, I could almost hear the faint strains of fairy music. It was my Piper-at-the-Gates-of-Dawn moment, as still and as enchanting in real life as I had imagined it when reading the book as a child.

In Finland, I learned why the Finns have a special feeling for trees: 'They are our church and our bank,' said Helmi, with quiet reverence. I also learned to forage for the canary-yellow chanterelle mushrooms, buried like bright jewels under the moss of the forest floor. Fried with a little dill on rye bread, they are beyond delicious. After Finland, I felt as if I'd been cleansed and scrubbed. I'd eaten healthy food, got plenty of exercise and been able to relax with regular sessions in the sauna. All this, and I'd acquired a new appreciation for the natural world. Finland had been restorative and it had left me feeling fresher and sharper than before. Whatever lay ahead for me in my Italian school, I was now in the right frame of mind to deal with it.

# CHAPTER NINE

# A CLASSROOM IN CHIANTI

The foreign language assistants in schools are usually odd fish. Outside of their natural habitat and transplanted into the noisy rhythms of a strange school in a strange country, they have a tendency to withdraw into themselves and can quickly become loners. Neither a teacher nor a student, they are betwixt and between; lost in that uncertain limbo between staffroom and classroom. Unless immediately adopted by at least one kindly member of staff, they are destined to roam the borderlands of school life for the duration of their stay. It's understandable. Adjusting to a new country and culture as well as the idiosyncrasies of the new school environment can be overwhelming, and other than being the school's resident foreign odd bod, they have little status.

In British schools, you can spot the language assistants a mile off. Their clothes, which are either terrifically stylish or hopelessly dowdy, are usually a dead giveaway; and they have an anxious, downcast look about them. Thinking back to the French assistants at my old school, from the young woman with the over-the-knee boots who gave us teenagers a titillating taste of French chic, to the fella who swanned about in a green velvet jacket and polo neck, they all seemed to have that same air of detached, moody resignation. It was as if they wished they were anywhere other than in a school where they were forced to listen to kids murder the French language. I like to think that in their real lives back in France, they were popular, fun-loving characters and that it was only British school life that wore them down to a parody of French angst.

Now here I was, about to take my very own brand of Black British angst into an Italian school, and knowing what I knew, I was braced for impact. I'd been assigned to a *liceo*, a senior high school, in Siena, which was about fifty kilometres south of Florence. As I prepared to assume my role as the dark outsider masquerading as an English language assistant, I felt like a gladiator about to step into the arena – primed, focused and fearless.

Of course, I'd been hoping for an assignment in Flor-ence, my old stamping ground, where I still had a network of friends and had developed all of my Black-girl-in-Italy survival skills; but the Central Bureau for Educational Visits and Exchanges based in London had other ideas.

Set into the soft undulations of the Chianti hills, Siena was a medieval jewel of a city that was loaded with jaw-dropping architecture and art and a history that could equal that of Florence. It was also the home of the world-famous Palio: the crazy horserace that took place twice a year right in the middle of the city. But with a population of just fifty thousand, Siena seemed like a provincial outpost compared with the bigger-city vibe of Florence that I was used to. Operating as a lone Black girl on this small-scale canvas was going to take every ounce of my resilience and ingenuity.

Friends, with more imagination than good sense, were already casting me as the female version of Sidney Poitier's character in *To Sir, with Love*, with the added frisson of my school being in the lavish setting of Tuscany rather than the gritty East End of London. Just like Sidney, my arrival in school would be met with initial shock and disbelief from both teachers and students. I'd get absolutely no respect in the classroom, where I would be the butt of crude pranks and sniggering jokes. Then I would come into my own. With my strength of character and my dark irresistible charisma, I would win my students over and take them on a journey of self-realisation as they blossomed into adulthood. I'd be like a superhero; a

Black Classroom Crusader who would not only subdue an unruly mob of white adolescents but I would have those delinquents eating out of my hand. By the time the credits rolled, I would have gained the admiration of my fellow teachers as well as the genuine affection of my students, who saw me as their role model and friend. There would be tears and fond smiles all round, maybe even an engraved tankard as a token of their affection.

It was a seductive narrative: compassion and decency triumph over ignorance and racism; although even I could see that *To the Signorina, with Love* didn't have quite the same ring to it. In any case, I knew better than to indulge in this kind of sentimental fantasy when it came to Italy. Still, in many ways, 'knowing better' was my big advantage. Unlike most of my fellow students who were coming out to Italian schools, I had plenty of first-hand local knowledge about Italy and Italian life. I'd already 'done time' there and wouldn't have to find my way about in the same way as they would. What's more, being an outsider was nothing new to me. Sometimes it felt like being an outsider was my full-time job. This year in school would simply be another version of it. I also knew that unlike the other English assistants, I would have issues of racial awareness to deal with; and in Italy that always meant going back to basics.

'Wait, *Signorina*! Wait! I think this belongs to you?'

I swivel round in the school corridor to see Beppe, the elderly janitor, scuttling behind me. The poor, old boy is breathless and he's brandishing something in the air, one arm waving in urgent semaphore.

'Look, *Signorina*. I found this. This big fork. It was on the floor in the staff room. Is it yours? I think it is. It was near where I saw you sitting with *Signora* Bramante. I picked it up and I said to myself, this must belong to the *signorina inglese*? Am I right? Is it yours?'

I'm confused. The man is rambling and I'm in a hurry to get to class. What big fork? What is he on about? It's then that I see that the 'big fork' he's wafting about is my tortoiseshell Afro pick. It must have fallen out of my bag when I pulled out my notes talking to Anna Bramante, the head of English, about the lesson plan.

'*Grazie, Beppe. Molto gentile.* It's a comb, by the way, it's not a fork. You know, *una pettine*.'

I do a comic little mime of combing my hair with one hand, but Beppe only looks baffled.

'*Che voul dire, Signorina?*'

A comb? What do I mean? You can't comb hair with this thing. It's clearly some kind of foreign implement for spearing or stabbing things. He's never seen anything quite like it. For all he knows, it could be a ritualistic object with magical powers or maybe some kind of talisman against bad luck. You never know with these people. They get up to all kinds of juju.

Instead of handing me the pick, Beppe now examines it more closely, like an expert handling an object out of a curio cabinet. I notice that some of the kids, who should be in their classrooms by now, are still hanging about in the corridor and they're starting to take an interest in the unfolding scenario. The new English (or so she says) *signorina* and old Beppe are having some kind of discussion and they can sense that there's an edge to it. Before we attract a small, interested crowd, I seize the pick from Beppe's hand.

'It's a comb. A *special comb* for *hair like mine.*' I say this with the kind of emphasis I use when I'm trying to explain an English phrase to the kids and they are slow on the uptake. Hair. Like. Mine. Get it? *Capelli come i miei.* I point my forefinger at my head like a gun. But Beppe's watery eyes blink at me blankly.

'A special comb, you say? But how exactly does it work, *Signorina?*'

What does he need? A demonstration? What I'd like to do is jab Beppe in the eye with the damn thing and tell him, 'There! That's how it works. How'd you like that? It's a special comb that doubles as a personal weapon. Now leave me alone, old man, and go about your business.'

Instead, I go to my failsafe response of the-well-meaning-foreigner-who-doesn't-quite-get-it. I shrug at him with a vaporous smile.

'How does it work? It works just like a comb. *Grazie, Beppe, grazie mille,*' I say, keeping up the same idiotic smile as I stow the pick away in my book bag. And with that I turn to walk off to my fifth-years conversation group. I know I leave Beppe gaping after me, as if I've just lifted a tantalising veil on some primitive ritual. But I can't help that. Right now I've got some irregular verbs to thrash out with the fifth-years and, anyway, shouldn't he be checking something in the boiler room or replacing a light bulb somewhere? Why is he forcing me to explain my personal grooming habits to anyone who cares to hear?

It's another cultural ambush foiled, but it always rankles. Although, to be honest, I had thought things had moved on with Beppe. I thought we had made some progress since my first day at school when he tried to sweep me off the premises like some undesirable.

I'd had to psych myself up to walk into the school that day, but no sooner had I crossed the threshold than Beppe leapt at me wielding a broom like a kendo warrior. It was a ruthless stealth attack and my only defence was a feeble yelp of surprise. Who did I think I was just wandering off the street into the school? Didn't I know this was government property? I was what? Sorry? Who? The new

English assistant who would like to see the head teacher? A likely story. Did I think he was born yesterday? Whatever I was pedalling, the school didn't want it, so I had better be off before he had the law on me. That's right. Go on. Honestly, these people! He shook the broom, as if to say 'don't make me use this'. It was a shocking start.

I'd been prepared for resistance. The leery looks and the cynical comments, and even the snorts of derision, were par for the course. I knew the drill and I was ready for it. But I could never have foreseen being threatened with the business end of a broom or being ordered off the premises like some vagrant. How had this sweeper of school floors got the power of say-so over me? How did menial Mr Mop-it-All have the right to judge me on sight and dismiss me out of hand?

When you mix blind fury with exasperation, indignation and shame, it becomes a powerful cocktail that helps you understand how the mildest of characters can be drawn to violence. Words become powerless. But instead of falling upon Beppe and beating him bloody with his own broom, I steeled myself to be still and be reasonable. I had no choice. I needed his validation to get in the building and do my job. It was only after I'd supplied the full name of the school's director as well as the head of English that Beppe relented with the broom and I was granted access to the premises – but only under his strict supervision. Yes, you could say that Beppe and I had come a long way since then. Over the weeks, he had become polite and respectful, rushing to open doors for me and sometimes even carrying my books; but there would always be setbacks, there would always be some fresh hell to deal with.

Foreign language studies often have a limited appeal for kids in school, and especially in the UK where they are seen as specialist subjects that attract a certain kind of student: girls, for the most part, who are not afraid to communicate and don't mind making the necessary mistakes in the process; girls who are destined to become modern language teachers themselves. But in schools outside the UK, it's a different matter. It's easy to forget just how much non-English-speaking youngsters really want to get to grips with speaking English. Not just the specialists, but all of them. English is the key to both American and British culture and more than anything, English dominates the international music scene, and this is the one language that most kids want to tap into.

No surprise, then, that whatever topic I would bring up in conversation classes, my students would invariably want to talk about music. They couldn't care less about how to describe weather patterns, ask for street directions or buy a train ticket in English. What they wanted to know was: who was best, David Bowie or Elton John? The Stones or the Beatles? Genesis or Pink Floyd? Or could I explain the lyrics to this or that song? It was assumed that I had an in-depth knowledge of the British and American music scene and that coming from England, I cared about it as much as they did. This sometimes led me down blind alleys that I had to back out of, as I trod a thin line between evasion and invention.

Today, we are talking about hobbies and favourite pastimes.

Lucia shoots her hand into the air. 'Yes, Miss. My favourite thing is to hear... *to listen* to the music of the Rolling Stones. I like this music very, very much. Please, Miss, what is a "honky-tonk woman"?'

I really don't want to teach fifteen-year-olds the English word 'prostitute', so I fake a mystified look and shrug, 'I'm not sure. I know that a honky-tonk is some kind of American bar.'

'So he is singing about a woman in a bar?' Lucia asks.

'Yes, I suppose so. A woman he meets in a bar,' I reply, thinking please don't ask me to translate any more lyrics from that particular song.

Thankfully, Stefano pipes up, 'I like the music of Jimi Hendrix, Miss. He is the best. I like the way he plays the guitar, Miss. Sometimes he is using his teeth. He is so... *selvaggio.*'

'Wild. Yes, that's the word you're looking for, wild,' I correct him, as I scrawl the word on the blackboard.

'Yes, I think he is… he *was* very wild. He died now. But he has hairs like yours, Miss. Jimi Hendrix has the same kind of hairs.'

'He *is dead* now. Dead is the past tense of "to die". And it's *hair*, Stefano. *Hair* not *hairs*.'

I quickly write all the parts of the verb 'to die' on the board followed by *hair (singular)* and *hairs (plural)*. I'm glad of a moment to divert the rest of the class from making a personal comparison between me and Jimi Hendrix, whose Afro always looked so rough and ready, either jammed into that suede fedora or swathed with a sweaty headband. Did he ever even comb it out? The same kind of hair? I don't think so. I don't play the guitar with my teeth and my hair looks a whole lot better than Jimi's scruffy Afro, thank you. So let's change the subject.

'Remember, it's singular in English. We *never* use the plural to describe the hair on our head,' I say, tapping the board authoritatively.

But then I think to myself: why? Why do we always use the singular in English? Underarm *hair*, facial *hair*, pubic *hair*. It seems to make more sense the way the Italians and the French say it in the plural.

It's only when you start to teach English as a foreign language that you begin to question it. Things you've never even noticed or have taken for granted suddenly don't make sense any more. Why do we say it that way?

Why do we spell it or pronounce it like that? How do we get 'taught' from 'teach' and 'bought' from 'buy'? You start to see and hear the language for the first time like a foreigner, and you are suddenly alert to all its complexities and quirks. When the kids look perplexed, you can't help but sympathise.

Meanwhile, Stefano is still in the Hendrix zone.

'What does "purple haze" mean? Is it a drug, Miss?' he persists.

'I'm not sure, perhaps...' I say, caught off guard, and mentally assessing a smooth exit.

'In this song, "Purple Haze", he is talking about kissing the sky, Miss. Do you think he was taking drugs?'

'Well, I don't know about that,' I say with a nervous chuckle. 'I only know a little about his music. But like you, a lot of his fans thought he was a very talented guitarist. *Wild* but *talented*? Do you know this word? It means clever, skilled, accomplished?'

I write all the words on the board, then in an attempt to shut down Stefano once and for all, I turn brightly towards another student.

'Now, is it Giorgio? I thought so. What's your favourite pastime, Giorgio?' I ask, hoping he'll turn out to be a model train enthusiast.

My fourteen- to eighteen-year-old students in Siena couldn't be further from the East End no-hopers that

Sidney Poitier's beleaguered character has to deal with in *To Sir, with Love*. They are all from well-heeled, local Italian families and they are studying towards their *maturità* exams in their final year. If successful, they will have access to university courses in architecture, medicine and law etc. Their parents are all heavily invested in their futures and most will be living at home with their families throughout their time at university. Less independent than British students, the young Italians nevertheless seem more mature and sophisticated. They have decided opinions and are fearless about expressing themselves and are generally much more politically aware than their British counterparts.

That said, of course, there is not one Black face among them, and they see me as some kind of freak of nature. While I have few discipline problems, the kids are as inquisitive as every other Italian to get to the bottom of me. They have no point of reference for racial awareness, as they never see anyone who looks like me, neither in school nor out. They struggle to match the visual reality of me with my role as an English language assistant in the school. They have a good idea of what the English assistant ought to look like, as they've seen my predecessors, and I don't fit the profile. Conversation classes can soon get personal if you don't keep your wits about you and I know that if I let them, they would bounce questions off me non-stop.

Which part of Africa are you from? Where are your parents being born, Miss? Are you American? Why are you studying Italian, Miss? Are you really English? No, but really? How can that be? Can you sing like Aretha? Can you sing like Donna?

Donna. In 1977, Donna Summer, the Black American disco diva, was a sensation in Italy. Playing across the country to capacity crowds of mostly Italian men, she was everything they believed a Black woman should be: hot, animalesque and uninhibited. Her stage presence was that of a beautiful and dangerous python, oozing, writhing and swooning with head back and eyes closed; Donna didn't just take you to the edge, she dragged you over the top into a freefall of sexual oblivion. Her guttural moans and prolonged sighs whipped Italian men into a mindless frenzy. Donna wasn't sexy; she *was* sex. Sex, on beautiful, long, brown legs; and she was hot and ready. In her two big hits, 'Love to Love You Baby' and 'I Feel Love', she simulated multiple orgasms so explicitly that her records were banned on many radio stations. One thing's for sure, I would never have to help the kids translate the lyrics for Donna's songs. There was no nuance of meaning in all those groaning 'oohs' and 'aahs' against the rippling beat of synthesisers.

I actually didn't mind her songs with the thumping bass, but her rampant stage persona, which was captured regularly on Italian TV, troubled me. It fed into that Italian macho mentality I knew too well, reinforcing the existing myths and beliefs about how Black women were generally perceived in Italy: Black women are available; Black women are hyper-sexual; Black women have got to have it. It was something I'd had to fight since my early days in Italy and it repelled and sickened me. Italian men were quick to sexualise most women at the best of times, but it was as if Donna had given them a special licence to see Black women as good for only one thing. I needed to put a distance between Donna's grinding stage antics and myself. Do I sing like Donna, they ask? No, I do not. Nothing about me is like Donna. Especially not my hair. Donna has fabulous long, free-flowing hair, which she flings back and caresses in sexual abandon. Her hair is a big part of her glamorous image. I don't have hair like Jimi Hendrix and I don't have hair like Donna Summer. But, then, I suspect that neither does Donna, and that those extravagant tresses go back on the wig stand at the end of each show.

The Donna phenomenon was all the more reason to channel a low-key, British vibe at the front of the class. I was dealing with impressionable youngsters with their hormones running amok. The last thing I wanted was to attract prurient interest or speculation about me based on nothing other than my skin colour. In the classroom,

I tried to be quietly spoken, measured and as neutral as possible. Ever-vigilant, I quickly discouraged any kind of over-familiarity in an effort to assert a professional distance between myself and the students. And if I came over as maybe a little prim and buttoned-down, that was fine with me. It was as much of myself as I was willing to put out there. I saw it as a matter of self-preservation. My teaching style was probably more *The Prime of Miss Jean Brodie* than *To Sir, with Love*, but it seemed to work anyway. Anna Bramante, the head of English, told me that the kids thought the new *signorina inglese* was '*troppo ganza*' – I was 'too cool'. I definitely wasn't trying to be cool, and I'm sure that just the fact of being Black accounted for some of the reputation, but maybe being a little standoffish helped to seal it. 'Too cool' – I could live with that.

Once I'd established my boundaries and won the confidence of students, I got a lot out of my school year in Siena. Thanks to Anna, I had a lot of support and guidance and she even trusted me to take some of the English literature classes. My inside experience in an Italian school gave me a new perspective on Italy and its education system and a sharper focus on what I wanted or didn't want for my own future. Unlike 'Sir' in *To Sir, with Love*, when it was time for me to leave, I was ready to go, and I did not discover my true vocation in the classroom. I'd enjoyed my stint in the school more than I'd thought I would, but it hadn't left me with a burning desire to teach. I knew I wasn't teaching material. I had neither the drive nor the passion for it, and these seemed to be minimum requirements for the makings of a good teacher. You can't fool the kids. They always know.

While the Italians were still drooling over Donna or hip-popping in the clubs to the Bee Gees with 'Stayin' Alive' and 'Night Fever', I got back to England to find not only that disco had become a dirty word but that disco was effectively dead. Not that I'd ever been a close follower of the music scene (despite what my students in Italy liked to think), but it was clear, even to me, that things had moved on. It looked like I had a lot of catching up to do.

I took a summer job in a shop in London before going north to finish my final year at university. After languishing for months in the Chianti hills, London felt alien and spiky. Punk rock was the new vibe and I just didn't get it. I tried to get it, felt that I ought to get it, but no: it just didn't take. Musically, socially, politically and stylishly, for the most part, it felt like being hit over the head repeatedly with a blunt object. This didn't feel like music for pleasure – more like music for punishment. And after the stylish chic I'd been inhaling every day in Italy, I found the studied grubbiness of the punk scene – all spiky hair, tattoos and safety pins – deeply unappealing.

While in London, I had a boyfriend called Mike, who was a social worker by day and a would-be punk at the weekends, when he fronted one of the many jittery, nerve-jangling bands that sprang up everywhere in the city. I tried to be supportive and went along to his gigs, usually in the sweaty smoke-traps of bleak upstairs rooms in pubs. If smart, socially conscious young men like Mike were getting something out of punk, then maybe I needed to somehow get on the inside of it. Maybe there was more to it than an angry energy that seemed to celebrate everything that was negative and nihilistic. 'It's rebellious, it asks questions and it's musical freedom,' explained Mike when I asked him for some clues. At heart, I was a soul girl, who had grown up on a steady diet of Tamla Motown and still had a lingering fondness for Stevie Wonder and Marvin Gaye as well as the powerful voice of Aretha Franklin. Besides, if it was about rebellion and asking questions, hadn't Marvin already done it so soulfully in his trailblazing album *What's Going On?*

I discovered that this was also the era in England of the 'two-tone' bands where Caribbean rhythms fused with punk rock and new wave in bands like the Specials and Madness. Mike was blond and blue-eyed and he was looking for a way to break into the London music scene. But when he suggested that the two of us should form an edgy 'two-tone' duo called 'Mike and Tina Turn-off', I had to laugh.

'I don't even sing,' I protested.

'That's the beauty of it. We don't have to,' he said simply.

I was still trying to get a handle on the British music scene, but I knew he was right. Neither one of us needed to sing. In fact, the ability to sing would be a definite disadvantage. With me Black and him white, we had the 'right now' look. I would rip holes in my tights, don a pair of army-surplus boots and comb out my Afro into mad, spiky tufts. If we looked mangy enough and could howl into a mic like a couple of injured tomcats, the bookings were bound to come rolling in. Did I miss my chance to make it big on the British music scene? Alas, I will never know as I turned Mike's offer down and headed back up north to face my finals. But I'll always wonder...

# CHAPTER TEN

# HAIR ON TRIAL
# IN AMERICA

My love affair with America took me completely by surprise. In 1980, fresh from graduating university, I arrived in Washington DC with a three-month visa and a sense that I was ready to 'do' America and then head right back home. A lot of my friends had done the same thing; taking any job they could get on arrival, usually in restaurants and bars, before using their earnings to hop Greyhound buses across states. Now they name-dropped New York, Miami and San Francisco into conversations as casually as they would Manchester and Leeds. How had I *not* been to the States? You must go, they urged me. You'll have a blast.

A prolonged spell in America was seen as a kind of finishing school, a rite of passage if you like, before we settled down to the real business of earning a living and taking

ourselves seriously. So as a recent graduate in Italian with
no fixed ambition, I was impatient to get the American
experience under my belt whatever it might turn out to be.
Yet it's fair to say that I was pretty phlegmatic about what
America might have to offer me after the lush superlatives
of Italy. How would America feed my soul? I'd lived in
Florence, for heaven's sake, where I'd been thoroughly se-
duced by everything from the language and art to fashion
and food, not to mention the men. At heart, I knew I
was a Eurosnob and I was convinced that three months
in this country of hamburgers, hotdogs and baseball was
long enough to claim more than a passing acquaintance
with America. I'd be able to add it to my life-experience
CV and move on. Job done. I arrived in America thinking:
*OK, let's see what all the fuss is about.*

So it was a shock to find myself swept off my feet and
getting giddy about all things American, from cocktails to
Cadillacs. The range of choices everywhere made England
feel like a provincial outpost where we happily shuffled
along with three TV channels and thought prawn cocktails
were the last word in fine dining. Here, when it came to
TV, you could go boss-eyed flicking channels between
crime shows, sport, comedy, news and religious revivals
where 'charismatic' leaders felt the spirit move them in
front of vast audiences. In just one block of the city, you
could eat Mexican, Japanese, Hawaiian or, armed with a

shell-cracker and steel pick, you could fight for your food, splitting a pile of fresh crabs at seafood restaurants. In fact, eating out often felt like you were entering a quiz show: 'Do you want Russian, Thousand Island, blue cheese, Italian, ranch-style, Caesar, honey mustard or vinaigrette dressing?' asked the perky waitress taking your order. And that was just the salad.

If Italy had wooed my senses, America walloped them like a shot of adrenalin straight into my veins. Suddenly, I was alert to something new in myself, an urgent pulse that I badly needed to tap into. It was as if for a long time I'd been sitting in a parked car with the motor idling and had suddenly been plunged into fast-streaming traffic on an eight-lane freeway. America was big, brash and crackling with possibilities and I desperately wanted to be part of it. In the land of All-You-Can-Eat, I was bibbed up and ready for a seat at the table. I was hopelessly bedazzled.

I set about an intensive familiarisation programme, exploring the shops in Georgetown, discovering the museums and galleries that lined either side of the majestic green swathe of the Mall and getting to grips with the transport systems. I started underground.

There was a futuristic feel about the sleek, clean lines of DC's Metro subway with its flashing discs at the platform's edge as trains approached. In the first few weeks, I rode the system back and forth on the same ticket, switching lines and savouring the station names: Federal Triangle, Foggy Bottom, Pentagon, Judiciary Square. I was in a thrilled kind of daze, but I tried to keep my cool. It was important not to give myself away by looking overawed by everything. I wanted to blend into my surroundings. It was on the Metro that I realised I'd never been in the midst of so many other Black people, who often outnumbered the white passengers in the cars. Like a spy dropped into a subterranean camp, I sucked up every detail, watching, eavesdropping and compiling my own intelligence report.

It seemed to me that Black Americans wore their Blackness differently to Black people in Britain. Here they moved and talked with the easy confidence of people who knew who they were and where history had brought them. I saw plenty of individuals with fabulous style and poise but also a lot of swagger and braggadocio. And so many shades of black – from polished blue-black and red-black to café-au-lait black and yellow-black. I would look around the car and realise that my skin colour actually didn't look out of place. After a lifetime of navigating predominantly white spaces, for once I didn't stand out like a black cat in a snowstorm. It was a weight that I didn't know I had been carrying and it felt good to let my shoulders drop and stand easy. I might not belong here, but at least it felt like I fitted in. And yet. I know I wasn't imagining it; I could see that something about me was drawing some quizzical looks.

Maybe it was my buttoned-down British-ness people sensed; the way I lacked the graceful fluidity of other Black people I saw around me. Or perhaps it was my unusual fashion choices that were drawing attention. At the time, I was channelling a retro-'40s look with a fitted burgundy gabardine, all sharp shoulders and deep buttoned cuffs. To complete the look, I was slicking back my unconstructed Afro and packing its springy volume into sequined and beaded hair nets in a big pouffe.

Thanks to Mamie's creative touch, I had come to prize the natural gift of my hair. I now knew what it was capable of and I was learning to have fun with it. I would sweep it all back or to one side or sometimes up into two Minnie Mouse-style pom-poms. I was looking after it better now too, oiling it and plaiting it up most nights then combing it out in the morning. This became a regular routine that made my hair softer and so much easier to manage as well as ensuring it kept its bouncy shape. Yes, I was enjoying playing around with it and expressing different moods and shades of my personality. I had definitely come a long way from those early years back in Yorkshire when trying to manage my hair had felt like a form of self-abuse.

'Say, where you from?' asked a woman with big, shiny bubble curls sitting opposite me on the Metro one day.

She had got on at Rhode Island Avenue and I'd noticed her eyeing me all the way to Silver Spring, where we both stood up to get off. The question was fired in a blunt staccato and for a moment I was taken aback. I was gathering my wits to answer when, as if suddenly wise to her own question, she said with a shrewd nod, 'New York, right? Yeah, I knew it. New York.'

The woman grinned, pleased with her powers of deduction, and she stepped off the train before I had a chance to open my mouth. She knew what she knew and my affirmation was not required. I watched her marching ahead of me along the platform, half wondering if I should catch her up and set her straight. But the truth is I was secretly rather pleased by her mistaken identity.

So that was it. I looked like one of those arty New York-types from the Woody Allen movies – an actor, a painter or maybe a writer. True, I couldn't remember seeing any Black people in *Annie Hall* or even *Manhattan* for that matter, but I told myself if there had been, they might have looked a lot like me. I liked this idea of looking interestingly off-beat and a little quirky. I was reinventing myself. I had no history here. I could be anything now. I would have to work this look, tweak it and perfect it. This would be my new American vibe – Black British boho. I had an exhilarating sense of my own, as yet undiscovered, potential.

Unlike other friends who had come before me, I always knew that being Black meant I'd have a different take on America to them. I knew that I would see things and be seen in ways that had bypassed their white British experience of America. For better or worse, my Blackness would be a visual statement sending signals ahead of me, signals beyond my control. In those early days in America while riding the Washington Metro, the incoming signals seemed to be bouncing off me like a radar station.

It looked like my British retro-chic was cutting a dash in conservative DC. At least that's what I thought at first. But it soon became clear that it wasn't so much my dress style as my hairstyle that was making people look twice. I could feel as British and boho as I liked, but this hair of mine was telling its own story; it was a story that puzzled Black Americans and they wanted to get to the bottom of it. All those side-long glances and wry smiles soon became vocal. It became a regular thing to find myself quizzed on the Metro or detained in shops or on the street by some random woman who *just had to* compliment me on my hair. Maybe it's the Brit in me, but I've never been good at handling compliments well, especially in public and especially from strangers. It's not about false modesty, because with each of these encounters, the Black girl in me was definitely flattered, only the British girl didn't really want a fuss. It felt like an invasion of privacy, as if someone was overstepping my boundaries. Murmured thanks and a polite smile were my usual response before quickly shutting the conversation down. It was nice to be noticed, but I didn't like being singled out and having to explain myself. It reminded me too much of all that unwanted attention in Italy.

But beyond my natural reticence, I was genuinely baffled. I honestly couldn't see what they were getting at. Were they blind? Didn't these women see that they had the same kind of hair as mine? The only difference was that my hair was in its natural state whereas they had gone to work on theirs with chemicals, hot combs, blow dryers and God knows what. But after a while, I was able to read the subtext of the compliments and understand why my hair was on trial every day in America.

'Honey, you got such *good hair*! Say, where you from?'

*Good hair*. What they really meant was that I had a terrific head of natural hair that was fantastic raw material to work with. What I had was the makings of 'good hair'. It was a great starter kit. It would look 'good' relaxed or 'good' relaxed and then permed. Didn't I know that I had the kind of hair and plenty of it that would straighten out beautifully with a good hot-combing session? What perplexed them was why I had left it like that. How come I wasn't desperate to get that stuff 'fixed' or 'processed' in some way or other? What on earth was I doing going around with all that hair

With my foster mother, Mary, soon after my arrival in North Yorkshire in 1957.

With my foster sister, Judith, in 1958. Yes, we *are* dressed up as golliwogs, ready to take the annual fancy dress parade by storm. Posing victorious by the sweet pea canes, we were thankfully too young to get the joke.

Me and Judith at a local fair, with Mary fluffing my hair. Mary's sister (*left*) was one of the 'frightening breed' of Yorkshire women who didn't quite approve of us.

Standing at the garden gate in my 'pinny', flanked by one of my foster father's old jalopies that he liked to build. Jack was also a keen amateur photographer, so it's thanks to him that these photos exist.

Frolicking on the beach at Scarborough. Was it ever really that warm?

For a few weeks at least, I was not only the darkest but the tallest member of my class at junior school.

ABOVE The Right School with the Wrong Hair. Pictured here at grammar school, in my second year, in 1967.

LEFT Thirteen going on thirty. Demure as a bridesmaid, with hair tamed, after a life-and-death struggle with spiky rollers.

BELOW After sixth form, I moved to Italy. The heat played havoc with my hair, so I resorted to the dreaded 'crisis crop'. Here I am larking about in the Boboli Gardens in Florence, with Linda, my in-house stylist, behind the camera.

Back from Florence for a friend's twenty-first birthday, rocking my new Italian style.

ABOVE After two years in Florence, I was ready to study Italian and drama at the University of Hull. Here I am playing it cool as First Fairy in the drama department's 1976 production of *A Midsummer Night's Dream*, with Sarah Greene, soon to be of *Blue Peter* fame, as Titania.

LEFT Hull again, channelling my inner Joan Armatrading, with a complex-and-misunderstood look.

After graduating, I headed across the Atlantic for a taste of America. This is me newly arrived in Washington DC in 1980, sporting a retro-'40s au naturel look, which so confused Black Americans, who had moved on to straightened hair and the popular Jheri curl.

I temped briefly in a mailroom before beginning work at the Italian embassy. Here I am at a presidential reception in 1981. My colleagues and I barely glimpsed President Reagan, but the food was wonderful.

One of the few pics of me with straightened hair. Here it is all glossy and floppy, with me hating it, at another embassy reception.

Dining with my old friend Bruce Oldfield while visiting London from DC, sporting one of my boxy cuts.

Eight months pregnant, celebrating the upcoming arrival of my child – a boy, everyone kept predicting – at my baby shower in Washington in 1983.

Shockingly, all the predictions were wrong: I had a beautiful little girl who shone like a jewel, Phoebe. Here I am with the Fabulous Feebs in DC in 1985.

Given my own childhood hair traumas, I struggled to manage Phoebe's curls. We fought a weekly battle with bobbles and barrettes.

LEFT When my church organised a tour of India, I jumped at the chance to explore a more spiritual path. This is me at the Taj Mahal, trying to imitate the winsome pose made famous by Princess Diana.

BELOW As well as providing wondrous sights, India presented me with unwelcome attention from kids who openly guffawed at my natural Afro, causing me to keep it under wraps for the rest of my stay.

The gollies reunited in Texas. With Judith in Houston on her wedding day in 2005. Natural Afro-Brit meets Afro-American chic.

Celebrating *Children in Need* in 2019 – a chance to act out a childhood fantasy of looking as cute and pious as Audrey Hepburn had in *The Nun's Story*, with my wimple hiding the hair I'd always been told was unsightly and troublesome.

One of the promotional graphics for my talks celebrating Afro hair that prompted me to write this book, designed by my friend, the cartoonist and illustrator Chris Duggan.

and just leaving it au naturel? Why wasn't I making the most of it? This is what the compliment meant when it was decoded. This was the big unsaid.

*Where are you from?* It's a question I can't hear without wanting to mentally roll my eyes. This again. It's a question I feel as if I've been answering to strangers all my life, whether at home or abroad. But in this American context of hair, I soon understood it to mean: where in the world is that kind of natural hairdo acceptable? Where do they still wear their hair like that? Was I from the Islands somewhere? Was I part of some religious sect? Or was I just some unsophisticated clod from the boonies who lacked city style?

'Thanks, I'm from England,' I'd say, hearing my own clipped consonants sounding a little stagey.

And it was interesting to see that this had an immediate effect. At the sound of my accent and at the mention of England, there would be a look of surprise, even disbelief. But the look quickly morphed into something like the shrewd nod I'd got from the woman who had nailed me as a New Yorker.

'OK. *Now* I get it,' said the nod; and they smiled at me indulgently. Of course. She's British. They hadn't thought of that.

Now my laissez-faire hair made some kind of sense. Britain was all kinds of crazy. On the one hand, it was punk rock and scrawny kids with bad teeth and safety pins through their noses. But then again, they had the Queen, didn't they? And what about all those highfalutin costume dramas you saw on the PBS channel like *Upstairs, Downstairs*? Britain was the 'old country' that revered the past. But it also had a nervy, radical edge to it. It was a place that managed to be classy and trashy at the same time. And where did a Black girl fit into this picture? Was it any wonder her style was so wacky and she didn't know what to do with that amazing head of hair? Now Black Americans were prepared to let me and my free-style hair off the hook. Now they were satisfied. I didn't know any better. I was just some crazy mixed-up Brit, they shrugged. Go figure. Being British demystified me for most Americans. It explained everything from my funny accent and my weird dress sense to my slack attitude to hair grooming. *She's British. No more questions, m'lud. The witness may stand down.*

In 1980, the Afro was dead in America. RIP. It had had its moment in the sun, and a splendid one at that. The Afro had defined a significant era in Black social and political history as well as in cultural style. Whether beautifully groomed on a *Vogue* spread or plain raggedy at some political rally, people looked back on it with fond nostalgia. Gone were the days when folks picked out their Afros to see just how big they could bush that thing out.

It had been a phenomenon that had crossed over from the radical arena of racial politics in America to become an international fashion statement. But nowadays, whatever way you styled it – flattened, tied back or swept into an updo – natural unadulterated hair like mine was a conversation piece in modern Black American society.

Now most Black women were using chemical preparations to either 'relax' their natural hair into straight styles or to perm it into the popular new style known as the 'Jheri curl'. This produced those loose, glossy curls and ringlets I'd been seeing everywhere on my Metro jaunts. I'd been intrigued by this style, which to my eye looked oddly unnatural and had a clammy sheen to it. But what did I know? I was just a Black British gal with no hair savvy. Thanks to music icons such as Michael Jackson and Lionel Richie flaunting their shiny new curls on MTV, the permanent wave that was the Jheri curl spread like a rash through Black America in the '80s. Men as well as women were mad for it. Curly swishability was the new straight and Americans loved it.

That Jheri curl was fierce. It involved a double blast of hard-core chemicals at one (very long) sitting. First, the stylist applied the pungent 'rearranging cream' to loosen the tight natural curl. Then came the heavy-duty perm solution. In other words, they had to straighten your hair out before they could curl it up.

You see, I was learning that in the world of Black Hair, there were 'good curls' and 'bad curls'. Bad curls were the natural springy coils we were born with, but good curls were what you got when you pimped it up with the Jheri curl. But if you wanted those loose, wet-look, even curls, they came at a price in both time and money. To start with, you had to be prepared to spend a day in the salon while various stages of the process 'took'. Achieving the Jheri curl was both time-consuming and labour-intensive and this meant it was a costly business. This was bad enough, but maintaining the look wasn't cheap either. After launching what amounted to all-out chemical warfare on your hair, daily applications of curl activators and moisturisers were essential to stop the hair drying out and becoming brittle and damaged.

And as Michael Jackson found to his cost while filming a Pepsi ad, some of those products were highly flammable. When a stray spark from stage pyrotechnics ignited the products in his Jheri curl, Michael lit up like a firebrand, suffering second- and third-degree burns to his scalp and face. There were similar stories of Black people becoming human torches when standing too close to lit candles in church. And all for the love of those shiny curls.

What I was learning was that Black hair was under siege in America. That most Black Americans were unhappy with the hair they were born with was evident in any drugstore you walked into. Here were entire aisles dedicated to nothing but Black hair products and haircare. Shelves were stacked with a bright and bewildering array of bottles, tubs, tins, sprays and box kits all aimed at combatting that stubborn kinky curl of Black hair: Sofn'Free, Dark and Lovely, Ultra Sheen, Afro Sheen, Care Free Curl, Curly Kit, relaxer kits for adults and milder relaxer kits for kids. Like everything else in America, there was an embarrassment of choice when it came to Black hair. It was as if Black people didn't believe in themselves with their natural hair. All it did was let them down. But somewhere among those endless rows of products was the miracle potion that would transform them; the prescription that would heal their damaged self-esteem.

Drifting between the shelves, I examined the gels, sprays, oils, creams and countless home kits, feeling like a tourist who was trying to pick up the local language. I may have been out of my depth, but even I could see how a multi-billion-dollar industry had grown up exploiting Black people's under-confidence about their natural hair.

You had to *kill* that kink. *Nuke it* with corrosive chemicals. *Burn it out* with hot irons and hot combs. *Blast it out* with the blow dryer. Kinky hair was the enemy that must be subdued at all costs, and America was waging an extremely lucrative commercial war against it. For women especially, keeping back the kink was a lifelong struggle, like rooting out weeds from the garden, you knew that stuff would always grow back so you had better stay on top of it. Somebody, somewhere – and you can bet it wasn't somebody Black – was making a killing from these products.

'Mercy! Look like you an' yo' hair 'bout to go on a peace march.'

This was Big Will, my manager, in the mailroom in DC where I got my first job temping. Coal-black and standing a gangly six feet and five inches tall, Big Will's loose-limbed walk was the confident sashay of a Black alpha male. Now he looked down on me benevolently as I sat flipping a stack of envelopes through a noisy franking machine.

'Ain't you heard, Li'l Sis? We emancipated now; an' we done pulled outta Vietnam a while back. Jeez! Even Bob Dylan's gone home. Man packed up his *gee*-tar and he be *gone*.'

Big Will chuckled to himself and lit another cigarette before settling on a high stool at one of the work counters as if he were ready to order up a round of cocktails at the bar. From this vantage point, I could feel him watching me with a mischievous twinkle in his eye. I was an oddball to him and I knew it.

Together with the real mailroom clerk, Chan, a milky-brown, freckled lad built like a wardrobe, I spent all day preparing packages and letters for a firm producing medical textbooks. I was still getting used to Big Will's rapid-fire 'jive talk', but there was no question that his perpetual wisecracking livened up the grunt work in the mailroom. With my compressed vowels and hippy hair, I was a rich source of inspiration for Big Will's rolling one-man show.

'Chan! Where you at? Come tell the sista here we *free at last*, or so the Man keep telling us.'

Unlike Big Will, Chan was too shy and good-natured to use me as a comedy punch bag. He simply wiggled the toothpick he always had clenched between his teeth and grinned. Whatever his thoughts, he kept them to himself, but it seemed that everyone else had an opinion about my hair that they needed to share with me.

An old Italian expression comes to mind; one of those ways of saying something in another language that is so precise you can actually feel, if not taste, its meaning.

*Non avere peli sulla lingua* means to be plain spoken, forthright. But what it is literally saying is 'not to have hairs on one's tongue'. And this makes so much sense because everyone knows that when you get a hair caught on your tongue, you can't help that fastidious tongue-flicking and dainty grasping at thin air with your fingertips in an effort to remove it. It's a delicate, slightly repugnant operation. So that *not* having hairs on your tongue means nothing is hindering you from speaking your mind. No reason to hold back.

And speak their mind they did. When it came to my hair, I was like a pheasant staggering clumsily out of the undergrowth at a shooting party. You had to take a pot-shot. After all, it was open season.

# CHAPTER ELEVEN

# HIDDEN ASSETS

I started to take a closer look at the Black women I saw around me in DC. The mailroom was situated in the basement of the building and sometimes I did the delivery run with Chan to the offices upstairs. Loading up the trolley, we took the lift to the first floor to distribute the incoming mail and pick up any outgoing. The first floor was a big typing pool full of mostly older women with just a handful of Black women among them. Chan was a favourite with all the women. Whistling quietly between his teeth while still swivelling that toothpick, he dished out the packages and envelopes while I collected from the 'out' trays. We had worked out a slick routine smoothly zigzagging up and down the rows of desks with a synchronised rhythm, but it was Chan that the women all welcomed with a smile. Did he want a cookie? What about some of that leftover birthday cake from yesterday? And how was his girlfriend doing?

I noticed that one of the Black women, Petra, had particularly lustrous hair. Shoulder-length and bone straight; she knew how to work it too. She tossed it away from her face with a practised flick of her head, giving Chan a cheeky wink as he handed her some letters. I wondered just how long it took her to achieve the look. How many hours in the salon? Or how many of those home-relaxing kits she needed from the drugstore? What were the tricks of her tresses? I also thought that if I had gone to the trouble of achieving such pretty hair, I wouldn't ruin its effect with that thick headband she always wore. It puzzled me, and I mentioned it to Chan as we came back down in the lift one day.

'What's with that big old headband Petra always wears? It really spoils her look.'

Chan's toothpick stopped mid-swivel and his eyes widened at me in disbelief.

'Serious? Are you for real? Hell, how else she gonna keep her wig on straight?'

Chan bent his knees and loosely clapped his hands as if I'd just fed him the punch line to a good joke. Spluttering with laughter, he could barely push the trolley out of the lift when we got back down into the basement.

Well, of course it was a wig. How had I not seen that? I

felt like an idiot for being so easily fooled. I suppose that until then, I had never thought about wigs as an everyday accessory. Wasn't there meant to be an element of subtle deception about wearing a wig? Surely you wanted people to believe it was your natural hair. If it was obvious to everyone, then what was the point? Chan had had no trouble spotting it, although that sturdy headband ought to have been a giveaway even for me. Face it. Your hair can be too perfect.

Sometimes it felt like every day in America was a re-education in Black hair culture. Black women in America, I was learning, often possessed a number of wigs as part of their essential wardrobe. They would get dressed, apply their make-up, then pull on a wig without a second thought. It was a quick and convenient solution that required none of the intensive grooming of their own hair. The wig was always ready to go. It occurred to me that they didn't really expect anyone, especially other Black people, to believe it was their own hair but just to admire the look they could achieve. Wigs let them ring the changes in style from day to day. I began to re-evaluate the interesting hairdos I'd been spotting – how many had actually been wigs? Yes, I could easily see how, in a busy lifestyle, the versatility and convenience wigs afforded made sense, but I did wonder if they were also another vote of no confidence in women's own hair; a cosmetic cover-up to hide the true nature of themselves. It was as if a lot of Black American women believed their own hair wasn't fit to be seen. No wonder my natural look was considered so unusual, so 'unnatural'.

Chan couldn't wait to tell Big Will how I'd been taken in by Petra's hair and they both chortled a little too loud and long for my comfort. The rest of the day, I caught them sneaking me pitying looks, as if they suddenly suspected I might not just be British but simple-minded with it. Later I saw Big Will jerk his head towards the ceiling as he murmured out of the side of his mouth to Chan, 'An' I bet she be hidin' a headfulla nappy hair under that fancy-ass wig upstairs.'

*Sotto voce* wasn't usually Big Will's style, so I knew I wasn't meant to catch this remark that he made with a smirking grin. It was for Chan's ears alone, just between the menfolk. It was another of Big Will's routine one-liners and the pair of them cackled like fellow conspirators; the way men do when they think no women are listening and they are getting away with it. I went on counting out batches of medical textbooks for the University of Southern California, glad not to be in on the joke.

I was mad at myself for being so gullible about Petra's wig, but I was prepared to take the ribbing. I deserved it. But I found Big Will's comment about her unjustified and mean-spirited. He was denigrating her natural hair as if it were something she ought rightfully to be ashamed of.

Something she needed to keep hidden. What's more, he was enjoying himself doing it. For all Big Will's relentless swagger and bluster, I liked him, but that sly remark stuck in my mind. It troubled me to think that even Black men could make Black women feel bad about their natural hair. No wonder so many women had lost their confidence in it.

'Nappy hair', they called it; or you were 'nappy-headed'. It was the first time I'd heard the expression, but I knew instinctively that Big Will wasn't paying the woman any kind of compliment. You never really heard it said out loud in the public arena, but among Black Americans, it was often said jokingly but nearly always with disparaging undertones. Just like that other 'N-word', it was a trigger word, rooted deep in the tragic history of slavery when Black people were regarded as no more than disposable property. I began to notice that Black people didn't mind tossing these words about among themselves ironically. As if by taking ownership of them, they defused their negative power. But I instinctively knew that using these words around white people was completely taboo.

Nappy hair was your natural, untreated Afro hair, with its tight texture of coils and kinks. But more than this, 'nappy' suggested that it was coarse, dry and unkempt. In fact, I'm pretty sure that growing up as a kid in Yorkshire, I could have been described as being nappy-headed. 'You can't be happy and nappy,' I heard other Black people say with a guilty chuckle. They didn't mean it. But then again, they did, as evidenced by all those anti-kink products in the drugstores.

I'd spent my life adapting my Blackness to a white world, but now I was being drawn into the codes and the behaviours of a Black culture that was entirely new to me. It had its own history, language, superstitions and beliefs; and it had its own private jokes. It was interesting to discover that many of these jokes reflected an ambivalent attitude towards one of their strongest identifying features: their hair. I soon became familiar with another phrase: 'Fried, dyed and laid to the side.'

This was a saying that gained currency back in the '20s and '30s, when many Black male entertainers got their kinky hair straightened out so that it could be smoothed (*laid to the side*) and waved into the fashionable white styles of the day. It was a look they knew made them more acceptable to white audiences in the sophisticated clubs where they were not accepted as patrons but only as performers.

A 'conk', as it was known back then, was achieved with harsh chemicals that burned (*fried*) the scalp and could do serious damage to your skin, especially when done on the cheap over the kitchen sink instead of at the barbershop. The longer you could bear to keep the toxic stuff on your head before rinsing it off, the straighter your hair would be at the end of the ordeal. It's sad to think that a towering musical talent wasn't enough. You had to put your audience at ease by mimicking its style. And getting rid of that 'other' kind of hair was the first step. Pictures from the time show some of the greats like Count Basie and Duke Ellington sporting hair that was unnaturally slick and shiny.

But that was all in the past. Things had moved on since then, hadn't they?

Or had they? If I'm honest, the more I looked around me, the more things didn't look so very different to me in '80s America, especially for women.

I saw that for any Black woman in the limelight, America was definitely a kink-free zone. No actor or entertainer would be caught dead flaunting her natural hair. Nobody needed to see *that*. Whether on stage or screen, the state of your natural hair was something you hid at all costs from the public; that was between you and your stylist or more likely you and your wig-maker. Straight was still seen as more attractive, more sexy and more powerful. In the fast-moving trends of the world of showbiz, wigs were often the quick-fix answer to instant glamour.

Things had moved on since the '60s when, in their identical evening gowns and stiff matching wigs, the Supremes harmonised 'Baby Love'. Their synchronised hip dips and graceful hand gestures did not ruffle one hair on those lacquered helmets. That big bouffant hair was especially reassuring to British audiences. It was showbiz hair just like Dusty Springfield's and Cilla Black's. It didn't get in the way of their sweet and sexy harmonies.

It took an act like Tina Turner in the '80s to take Black wigs from reassuring to raunchy. Her big wigs went from dead straight to spiky-straight, in keeping with her new image as a rock chick who could hold the stage with rock icons like Mick Jagger and David Bowie. Tina's wigs had natural movement and were part of her high-octane performance as she tore up the stage thrashing her hair about like a wild cat with its tail on fire.

Whitney Houston's wigs were more feminine and conservative, but in her perky dance video 'I Wanna Dance with Somebody', she whipped about a head of long blonde curls that infuriated some in the Black community who were quick to label her 'not Black enough'. Black hair, real or false, was a sensitive topic that could stir up strong feelings around racial politics. In the Black entertainment world, God forbid that you tried too hard to cross the line into white acceptability. It was a dilemma for a lot of Black artists trying to make the crossover to a white audience. How far did you go? After all, you might not be able to change your skin colour (though some did try), but there was no doubt that changing your hair texture would certainly help, just like the conk had done all those years before.

And then God created Oprah. It was the '80s that saw Oprah Winfrey's meteoric rise as a multimedia phenomenon that has yet to be surpassed. Here was a woman who didn't have to worry about attracting a crossover audience; the whole world loved her. Her voluminous hair that went through a succession of weaves, wigs and hot presses was as hot a topic as any of the burning questions of the day discussed on her show. What products did she use? How often did she wash and condition? Was it a weave or natural? Her audience, both white and Black, wanted to know how a Black woman managed to pull off such glamorous and enviable tresses. What was her secret? As the undisputed Queen of Daytime TV, Oprah had no qualms in publicly admitting that her hair was out of her hands and completely under the control of a team of top stylists and consultants.

Next to Oprah, Phylicia Rashad was probably one of the most famous Black female faces on TV in the '80s. In her role as the attractive lawyer and wife in the hugely popular *Cosby Show*, her hair was always styled sleek and straight with nary a kink in sight. It was shiny and bouncy and as unprovocative as Black hair can be. Everything about Ms Rashad's hair suggested she was wholesome and commendable as the girl next door. You couldn't take exception to it. It had the same effect as those lifeless wigs the Supremes used to wear twenty years before. It was reassuring and it put people at ease. She was Black all right, but she was 'safe'. You might even think that her hair grew naturally that way if you hadn't seen pictures from her early career showing her rocking her natural Afro.

You had to wonder what it was about our natural hair that was so contentious and provocative. Why did we feel the need to apologise and make excuses for it? Why must we transform it or hide it altogether? And why was it so stigmatised not only by those of us who were born with it but by those who weren't?

# CHAPTER TWELVE

# SHIFTING GEARS

Meanwhile, America continued to beguile me. I still saw riding the Metro as my essential training ground where I watched, listened and filed mental notes to explore at my leisure. One of my favourite stops was Smithsonian, where a dizzyingly steep escalator spat me out onto the wide-open stretch of the Mall. Gliding up from the cool shadows of the subway, I felt like Botticelli's *Venus* on the half-shell rising from the cavernous deep into the glorious sunlight of my future, with flowers at my feet and the gentle breeze of Zephyr at my back. Before me was the great white dome of the Capitol and behind me, the soaring needle of the Washington Monument poked uncompromisingly into the sky. Surrounded by these symbols of power and achievement, it wasn't hard to reimagine myself as someone special and privileged; someone destined for greatness. It was the perfect backdrop for entertaining heroic fantasies of conquering America. I was at large in the Land of the Free and the Home of the Brave, and I was determined to learn every single word of 'The Star-Spangled Banner'.

I came into the mailroom one day to find Big Will jabbing a long bony finger at the classified ads he was reading in the paper.

'Check it out, Li'l Sis. This here's a job that you just might could git. Alls you gotta do is let 'em hear some o' that fancy-ass talk o' yours.'

I peered dubiously at the ad that had got his attention and I shrugged. Big Will's 'just might could' seemed to sum it up. It was a long shot all right. I doubted that my English accent made any kind of impression outside the mailroom, but then again, I seemed to have the basic qualifications. What the heck had I got to lose? I didn't mind the repetitive drudgery of the mailroom, all the packing and weighing and stamping while Big Will railed about the 'jive-turkeys' he had to deal with upstairs, but I knew it for what it was: a backroom job behind the scenes that made absolutely no demands on my intellect. The real America was still out there waiting to be conquered and the mailroom was beginning to feel like a cop-out, a safe house where I was lying low. If I was going to have any kind of future here, I was going to have to go out and chase it. What was I afraid of? What was holding me back? I needed to start putting myself out there; find a job that didn't involve wearing crumpled Levi's and a pair of scuffed trainers. A job I could sink my teeth into.

Big Will's finger tapped the ad insistently, forcing me to read it again: 'The Embassy of Italy requires bilingual Administrative Assistant.'

This was clearly a job aimed at Italian Americans. Besides, it seemed like a big leap from mailroom lackey to the world of international diplomacy; but Big Will's finger kept on tapping. There was no way he was going to let it go.

When I got the job, I felt as if I'd won the lottery. But as Big Will told anyone who would listen, it was no surprise to him. No way, José. He knew it all along. Hadn't he hand-picked the job out for me his *own* self? But for him, I'd still be bustin' my hump packing books same time next year.

'What I tell you, Li'l Sis!' he crowed from one end of the packing room to the other. 'Who the Man with a Plan? Huh? Who got the goods? Big Will that's who. You hear me, dontcha? Sooner you git your British *bee*-hind outta here, sooner you be making boo*koos* o' dough. I'm talkin' those *big bucks*. You better keep on steppin', Li'l Sis.'

The new job called for an abrupt change of gear and an entirely new perspective. After the shambling pace of the mailroom, I was plunged headlong into the fast and focused routine of a busy press office in the international sector. Now I was in the thick of it. Now I spent my days fielding calls from Congressional aides, contacting journalists, drafting press notices and making reservations at the Kennedy Center. The *Washington Post* and the *New York Times* became the twin Bibles that I lived by; monitoring them daily, I soon knew the names of editors and staff writers and had direct lines to their PAs. It was a dream job and what's more it came with a built-in visa. I had to keep stopping to remind myself. Look at me. I'm on the big stage now. I'm part of the motor that drives events in Washington. Thanks to a timely shove from Big Will, of all people, I'm finally in the mix. I was thrilled and I was terrified.

In getting this job, I felt more than lucky; I felt chosen. It sometimes felt as if Big Will had been my fairy godfather, magically plucking the job out of thin air. Yet it couldn't have been further away from the laid-back rhythms of the mailroom.

It was a role that plunged me into the very heart of cultural and political life in the nation's capital and I was relishing every moment of it. When I wasn't liaising with the press and departments in the federal government, I was hanging around the edges of high-profile events such as gallery previews, press conferences, business lunches and diplomatic dinners. It was exciting having a front-row seat, and while I was a long way from Big Will's prediction of making those *bookoos* of bucks, I didn't care, because I was definitely getting *bookoos* of experience working in an environment I could never have imagined. Now all I needed was to start looking the part of a professional woman with prospects. I needed to update my image to match the job.

Myrna, one of the older Black women I worked with, decided to take me under her wing. She had once been new to DC herself and I sensed that she saw this awkward young Black girl with the unlikely accent as something of a project. As my unofficial mentor, she talked me through the politics of survival in the DC office environment, which included how to manage the outsized egos of some of the bosses and when to avoid the break room. She took an interest in my personal life too, recommending places to shop and eat and clubs where she believed I was more than likely to meet (if I hadn't already) 'some fine-ass man'. There was just one thing...

'Say, honey. What we gonna do 'bout your hair?'

Sounding like a concerned mother who only wants the best for her girl, Myrna cast sorrowful eyes over my hair. I suspect she'd been holding fire for as long as she could, because although I was still the new girl, I'd already heard the whispers. 'Don't mess with Myrna' was part of the unwritten office code. She was the tiger you wouldn't dare try to ride. I knew that she was an advocate of the 'tell-it-like-it-is' school of behaviour. Those 'no-hairs-on-the-tongue' Italians had nothing on her.

I might be the new girl, but I let her know that I was no pushover. I held my ground proudly and stood up to her. Without flinching under Myrna's punishing gaze, I told her that I liked my hair the way it was, thank you. It's true, there had been a time when I'd had to work hard to accept it, but now, guess what, I was completely in synch with my kink. I loved it and I was proud of it. I didn't see it as a cause for concern and I assured her that I had no plans to 'do' anything with it.

I was pleasantly polite, but I was firm. And it seemed to have worked, because Myrna simply kissed her teeth and shrugged. *Whatever.* It was all the same to her. With some relief, I felt the little knot of tension loosen between us as she turned towards the door of the press office. I sure as hell didn't want to mess with Myrna, but I wasn't about to be cowed by her either. It was then that I saw her lingering by the door with a pained smiled: 'Hey, I'm just sayin', hon. That hair of yours is *so '70s.'*

There it was: the unadorned, unvarnished truth according to Myrna. She knew how to deliver the sucker punch; how to hit a vital nerve. Without another word, she wandered off back to her office and I spent the rest of the day with her damning utterance playing on repeat in my head.

In any case, I knew that wasn't the end of it. As if.

Myrna was an old campaigner. She wasn't known for backing down from a little resistance. If anything, it only whetted her appetite. This had merely been her opening salvo, a warning shot over my bows. Me and my hair were now firmly in her sights. I was a marked woman. She was coming after me.

Myrna knew I was desperate to fit in and make a success of the job. With a few choice words, she let me know that my Afro-Brit vibe might be OK for the student campus, but it wasn't cutting it in professional America. In fact, she hinted, it was probably holding me back. But it had been her last throwaway remark – '*so '70s*' – that had hit home hard. The idea of being thought of as outdated and unfashionable had struck a painful chord and, subtly at first, my thinking began to change. Why jeopardise my chances? What was the big deal anyway? It was only hair after all. I wasn't losing a limb. I'd got this far, so was I really going to risk future opportunities for the sake of the wrong kind of a hairdo? With relaxed hair, I would look more polished and business-like. Sure, I'd look different. But I *was* different now.

I'd already ditched my retro-'40s look, swapping it for a more conservative, classic style like the ones I'd observed on the Metro. These were usually fitted two-piece suits or tailored skirts and blouses worn with trainers for the commute and switched for sensible heels in the office.

The pinch and squeeze of my student days suddenly felt a long way behind me. Hell, I had credit cards now, shopped at Bloomingdale's, hung out at bars in Georgetown and ate at Red Lobster and Benihana. With Americans, I already knew better than to interrupt any talk about the Redskins' chances for the Super Bowl, although I could sing 'Hail to the Redskins' with gusto along with the best of them. What's more, I never missed an episode of *Soul Train* on TV, whooping along with the on-screen crowd as the dancers strutted their stuff to Shalamar and Earth, Wind & Fire. It was more raw and funky than *Top of the Pops* back home, where the in-studio audience seemed to do little more than dither about half-heartedly to ABBA. The Black dancers on *Soul Train* weren't afraid to get down and dirty with the beat, showcasing their individual style in slick, synchronised moves. And there were no hyped-up DJs yelling into the mic on *Soul Train*, just the rich baritone of the ever-suave Don Cornelius, creator and presenter of the show. It was amazing to think I was living and working in a city with its own Black university and I loved listening to all the Black music on WHUR, Howard University's own radio station. Face it. I was a complete convert to Team America. I no longer felt like an outsider looking in.

If relaxing my hair had once felt as radical as plastic

surgery, it now began to feel like a natural part of the adventure, another step towards self-development now I had money and options. I owed it to myself to take things to the next level. De-kinking my hair would complete my Americanisation.

Myrna was too smart to keep hammering away at the same old nail. Instead, she adopted the crafty strategy of omission. She would compliment me lavishly, praising my cute accent, my outfits, my jewellery, my shoes, my make-up but reserving no more than a long-suffering sigh for my hair. Such a pity. That hair of mine was crying out to be taken in hand.

Even now that I was feeling more adventurous, I still chose my moment carefully. One day, dropping off notes from a meeting in Myrna's office, I turned to leave and asked, in a 'Oh, by the way' kind of tone, if she knew of a good home-relaxing kit that I might try out.

'*Home kit? Try out?*' Myrna's eyebrows shot north. 'You're kidding me, right?'

She got up quickly from her desk, cutting off any ideas of a swift exit by firmly closing the door. She'd been waiting for this. She was locked and loaded.

'Say, why you want to go messing with all that DIY stuff? Besides, there's no telling how it'll turn out. You gotta do it right. You gotta go to a professional. Someone

who knows what they're doing. You ought to go see Raphael downtown. Man's been fixing my hair since for *ever*.
He'll take care of y'all.'

There was no denying that Myrna's hair always looked
good. She wore it straightened in a stylish pixie cut that I
knew was all her own hair. Eager not to lose momentum,
she was ready to phone and book an appointment with
Raphael on the spot, but I thanked her and said I'd like to
think about it.

'Don't go thinking for too long and don't go trying any
of that home kits foolishness, you hear? You got to know
what you doing,' she warned darkly.

I wasn't just playing Myrna; I really did need to think
about it. The thing is I hadn't forgotten the last time I'd
been in a hair salon. How could I? The ghost of Rodolfo
back in Italy still haunted me; the way he had dismissed
me with such dignified scorn and the way I had backed off
into the street feeling like a leper. The man had made me
feel as if my hair was a punishment to look at let alone to
touch. Even the tender words and caresses of Marco had
not had the power to heal that old wound. I still shrank
from the memory, and my faith in hairstylists had never
recovered.

But now Raphael. Mmm. I won't pretend that I wasn't
intrigued. After all, it *was* the name of one of the great
master painters of the Renaissance; the man who had

given Michelangelo himself a run for his money. You had only to think of the timeless serenity of some of those exquisite Madonnas Raphael had painted. Hey, I could be timeless. I could be serene. Why not?

And wasn't Raphael the name of an angel, a guardian of travellers and pilgrims and a healer? Surely these were all good omens. Here I was on the road to a better version of myself and I was in the company of artists and angels. There was no telling what divine transformations *Raphael downtown* might create with my hair. At last, I could move on. I could put the dark shadow of Rodolfo behind me. Raphael was the man for the job. I was sure that I would emerge out of his salon a new woman. It was time, I told myself. It was time to go straight.

# CHAPTER THIRTEEN

# THE SHOCK OF THE NEW

'**G**ood hair doesn't happen by chance; it happens by appointment' read the sign in the window of Raphael's salon. It was a much-needed boost to my confidence, which had been draining away on the bus journey downtown. I was getting cold feet and I'd been wondering at what point I could still change my mind. Yes, I wanted to fit in, but how far must I go? Did it really depend on me changing the entire texture of my hair? Would it really make a difference?

But anyway, here I was, and there was the man himself. Raphael, Hair Alchemist Extraordinaire. Of course, in reality, Raphael was no angel. In fact, he was a faded little French Canadian whose own hair was fast becoming a memory. His personal hair credentials were saved by an elaborate beard and twirled moustache arrangement, which from time to time he gave a dandified tweak.

Once Raphael had cranked me up in the chair in front of the mirror, I knew there was no turning back. He began to give my hair a thorough workout with his hands. He parted it in the middle, scraped it back from my forehead, then raked it up from the nape of my neck. He tried combing it through from the roots with his fingers but met immediate resistance in the complex tangle of coiled hair. So now he grabbed it in bunches, twisting the ends around his fingertips as if trying to read its springy behaviour, predict what it might do. Finally, he began tugging my hair out in uneven tufts all over my head to get the measure of its full thickness and length.

Seeing myself in the mirror looking like a close relative of Worzel Gummidge didn't feel like a good start. Raphael puffed out his cheeks in a deep sigh, as if to say it was going to take all his professional skills to pull this one off. For a moment, I feared I was going to be shown the door with a repeat of Rodolfo's *gran rifiuto*. I held my breath, not sure if I would be more relieved than humiliated a second time around. Instead, Raphael stood back with one finger crooked thoughtfully under his chin, deliberating the task that lay ahead.

'Madame, the problem eez we 'ave *too much* 'air. First, we *theen it out, non?*'

He sounded a little frustrated, as if Myrna ought to have warned him of what he'd be up against when she made the appointment for me. I shrugged. Sure. Go ahead. Thin it out. What did I know? He was the professional. I was just some unstylish British gal looking at him in the mirror like a depressed scarecrow. Raphael began hacking at my hair like a man on a mission. I tried not to look with dismay at the mounds of hair that began littering the floor around me in fluffy, dark clouds. I wished that I knew some relaxation techniques that would stop me digging my nails into the arms of the chair.

Once he was satisfied with his pruning, Raphael plastered a white paste over my hair.

'It feels kinda funny,' I said, forcing a smile through clenched teeth. 'Is it meant to feel this way?'

'Funny, madame?'

Raphael raised his eyebrows, but there was a testy edge to his voice and his shoulders seemed to stiffen a little.

Was I questioning his professional expertise now? Me, the clueless client who had presented him with a head of hair so thick he'd been forced to hack it back like an explorer cutting a path through the jungle. He'd had to thin the stuff out before he could even make a start. Now what? It feels kinda funny? What was my problem?

'Oh, you know,' I went on, losing confidence by the second. 'Kind of warm and tingly.'

'That's good, madame. That's normal. It's just the relaxer working its magic,' Raphael patted my shoulder like a kindly uncle and gave me a strained smile in the mirror. 'Believe me, madame, you are going to look like one sophisticated lady when you walk out of here.'

He checked his watch and slid away to manage one of his more savvy clients – the type of client who understood about suffering a little for their beauty; the type who didn't start wriggling and whinging when their head began to warm up like a hotplate.

I believed him. But this white gloop he'd smeared over my hair under the plastic bonnet not only felt funny but it smelled funny too. It looked like shaving cream, but it was giving off a decidedly foul smell; it hung about me like a lingering fart that everyone is too polite to acknowledge. It smelled bad and it felt weird. But here I sat with my hair pasted to my head with stinky gloop waiting for a miracle. I reminded myself that I was on the verge of a major image change. My transformation from a 'laid-back' '70s chick with a natural hairdo to a 'go-getting' '80s gal with sleek, well-coiffed hair was just around the corner. On the other side of this noxious smell and the prickly heat crawling over my scalp, I was ready to meet the new me. Sure, I was feeling a little warm and whiffy, but this was no time to lose my nerve. I believed, like Raphael said, that what I was feeling was the magic potion at work. Bibbidi-bobbidi-boo! Why lose faith now? All I had to do was sit back and let the chemistry happen while resisting the urge to scratch at my head like a flea-ridden mutt.

I had to sit waiting for the concoction on my head to 'take', and while I riffled through back copies of *Vogue*, I tried not to think of some of the horror stories I'd heard around using relaxers: chemical burns, scalp scars, permanent hair loss, migraines and breathing problems. But I quickly reassured myself: these women were more than likely doing it on the cheap at home with one of those drugstore box kits that Myrna had warned me against. Some women had no other choice but to DIY it and take the risks that came with it. That's why I was paying top dollar in the safety of a sleek, professional salon like Raphael's, but I also realised that, unlike many Black women, I now had the spending power that made this possible. A box kit? I could still see the scowl of disapproval on Myrna's face. She was never going to let that happen. Not on her watch.

I was beginning to think that my head was actually going to burst into flames when thankfully Raphael nodded one of his assistants over to rinse out my relaxer. I was glad to get my head under water and feel the heat being rinsed away from my scalp, although I noticed that the shampoo didn't smell too good either. Instead of the usual fruity or botanical fragrance wafting back at me, this stuff gave off an ammonia-like whiff that settled in my nostrils. I knew this was the neutralising shampoo that deactivated the relaxer and that a revolution was taking place on my scalp as chemicals fought chemicals. To take my mind off this, I focused on the soothing slosh and gurgle of the running water; I told myself it was washing the old me away and down the drain. I was about to rise like a glamorous phoenix out of the smoking ashes of my past.

Myrna wasn't alone; most Black women I met couldn't believe that in my mid-twenties I was still a relaxer virgin. For them, it had been an early rite of passage. Braids, cornrows and plaits were for kids, but once they got to a certain age, often as young as nine or ten, they had had their first relaxer. You could say it was an initiation into womanhood. And there was no doubt that it made your hair easier to manage, but you knew, without anyone spelling it out, that straightened hair was the minimum requirement to acceptance in what was essentially a white world out there. Of course, you weren't forced to relax your hair, but like getting a driver's licence, you'd be mad not to. And so began the cycle of relaxer dependency. Just like a drug, you were hooked on a habit that cost a fortune and could last for decades. No wonder Black American slang for relaxers was 'creamy crack'.

Two more shampoos and a deep-conditioning treatment and I'd been clipped, slathered, lathered and rinsed until my scalp felt raw and squeaky. Between each operation, I was left to my own devices for long periods of time and I was sorry that I hadn't brought along a book. Lulled by the drone of hairdryers, there was nothing to do but flick half-heartedly through the pages of *Vogue* and *Harper's Bazaar* while sipping cups of tepid coffee. Apparently, the new look was power suits teamed with big, clunky jewellery. The tailored suits had shoulder pads wide enough to claim their own postal zone and the big, pearl-studded crosses dangling everywhere looked more cumbersome than stylish. I began casting wistful looks towards the door of the salon. Four hours in and I was starting to feel like a trapped animal. I was bored now and rapidly losing interest in what was to become of me and my hair. I just wanted to get outside and breathe some fresh air.

By the time Raphael beckoned me back onto the swivel chair, I was grateful, at last, to be on the home stretch. The first thing I noticed was that Raphael's comb went straight through my damp hair, which for the first time lay limp and flat against my head. Usually, when damp, my hair shrinks and falls into loose corkscrew curls that need an Afro pick to carefully separate and lift them. But Raphael's comb – and a normal comb at that – slipped through my hair like a knife through butter. There was absolutely no resistance. For the first time since entering the salon, I felt a twitch of excitement. I'd often tried to imagine what this must feel like; combing my hair with straight, easy strokes had been a childhood fantasy, and it was an experience I'd never had. This promised a whole new relationship with my hair, and I suddenly realised that I didn't even own a regular brush and comb. Until now, I had never had any use for them.

Raphael combed, blow-dried, primped and sprayed. Yet I found that I daren't focus too closely on what was actually going on in the mirror. I knew I still wasn't ready for the Big Reveal. Instead, I concentrated on Raphael as he fluttered around me like a ballet dancer confident of his own artistry, as he titivated with fingers and combs and clouds of hairspray. I noticed the G buckle on his smart Gucci belt and I liked the way his gold bracelet glinted under the harsh salon lighting. Somewhere behind the drone and babble of the salon, I could hear the intermittent squeak of what sounded like Vivaldi and I closed my eyes and tried to attune my ears to the music; anything to take my mind off that blasted mirror in front of me. Then, with a magician's flourish, Raphael whipped off my plastic cape with a dramatic swoosh.

'Et voilà, madame!'

I admired his showmanship, even though I didn't feel equal to it. Instead, I glanced dutifully at the image in the mirror and gave Raphael a sickly smile before sliding off the chair. One of the assistants found my coat as I coughed up $80 at the front desk without a murmur.

Avoiding the mirrors in a hair salon is a neat trick if you can do it. But if you stare hard enough so that your eyes actually become unfocused, believe me, it can be done. I somehow couldn't bring myself to come face to face with the new me in the salon. I knew I was going to look very different and I was afraid of my reaction, whatever it might be. In true British fashion, I was reluctant to show an excess of joy or disappointment in public. Whatever the outcome, it seemed a private moment, not something to be shared with strangers.

Five hours after setting foot in the salon, I was released back into the wild. Outside, I could feel my hair lifting slightly in the breeze and loose wisps falling into my eyes; sensations that felt shockingly alien. It was only now that I felt free to examine my reflection in a shop window. So this was the new me. The American version. The woman staring back at me had a tiny head and a big face. Her hair seemed almost incidental. She was a stranger to me. Nervously, I ran my hand through my new hair. Just like Raphael's comb, it met no resistance but slipped easily through the strange, silky stuff I now had on my head, which flopped immediately back into place. I looked harder at my reflection, trying to recognise myself. *You'll get used to it*, I told myself. *You'll get used to it and you'll love it.*

'Relaxed', they called it; more like my hair was in a coma. When I got my new hair home, like a paramedic at the scene of a bad accident, I did everything I could to try to resuscitate it. I raked through it repeatedly with my fingers and my Afro pick in an effort to plump it up again. Panicked, I then tried to backcomb it into some kind of shape, but I just ended up looking like a mad cockatoo. In desperation, I ran to the drugstore and for the first time in my life bought hair lacquer ('super-hold') in an attempt to stiffen up the texture and give it some shape and height. But it was all useless. The chemicals in the relaxing cream had completely re-programmed my hair. It used to have more body than Mr Universe, but now it just lay there playing dead. I couldn't believe it; this stuff used to have so much fight in it, but now, like a punch-drunk boxer, it was out for the count. *You'll get used to it*, I told myself with less and less conviction. I never imagined how much I would miss the volume and the control of my natural hair.

I could have wept when I thought of all the hair I'd left lying on the salon floor destined for the trash. Why had I let him do it? Master stylist? The man was a master hair criminal. Pure and simple. I felt like the newly shorn

Samson and I didn't know whether to cast Raphael or Myrna as the Delilah of the piece. All I knew was that with my hair gone, I felt physically and emotionally weakened, as if I'd lost all of my strong definition. And just look at my face. It was out there now. Who knew that my nose was so wide or that I had the jawline of Desperate Dan?

Honestly? I was in shock. I can't tell you how much I hated my new hair right from the start. Funny thing was that everyone else positively raved about it. Friends Black and white seemed to be relieved that I had 'normalised' my hair at last.

'Now *that's* what I'm talkin' about! *Giiirl!* Look at you! You look so *fly!*'

Hands on hips and head to one side, Myrna stood back admiring my new hair as if it were all her own work.

'That hair of yours! Well! It was a crying shame. But just look at you now! Didn't I tell you Raphael would do a real good job of it? Now that, *right there*, is your look. Come on now. You got to admit that's a *whole lot better*, and I know you *feel* better too, don't you? Sure you do. Hey, Sandro, Lina, how d'ya like our new girl now? Isn't she somethin' else!'

Myrna was delighted. I was her personal triumph. The sow's ear had become a silk purse. She would have paraded me through all three floors of the office if I had let her, but I reminded her that I needed to get started on a round of phone calls for the upcoming press conference at the State Department. My victory lap would have to wait.

'You look more streamlined,' remarked one colleague approvingly, as if I were a study in aerodynamics.

'I know you feel better too,' Myrna insisted. She was wrong. I didn't feel better. I felt a whole lot worse. And 'Isn't she somethin' else?' she had cooed, drawing the others in the office into the big hair conspiracy. And she was right about that at least. I was 'somethin' else'. After all those years of wondering what I would look like with straight hair, well now I knew. I looked like somebody else. That's all. It wasn't me. That woman in the mirror was a bad impersonation of the real me. She looked like an alien. I couldn't warm to her.

'You just have to get used to it,' friends kept reassuring me. But I didn't want to get used to it. I had been the victim of undue influence. I'd been coerced, bamboozled.

'Mind,' said Myrna, wagging a warning finger in my big face. 'You have to stay on top of it now. You need to go see Raphael every six weeks to keep it in good shape.'

Sure, I nodded affably. *Like hell*, I thought. I had no intention of letting that Canadian hair thief anywhere near me again. In the meantime, I would have to play along with this new hair with as much grace as I could muster. I would learn to accept the compliments and agree amiably when people mentioned that it must be *so much* easier to manage. Easier to manage; I heard this so often that I knew it wasn't just about the practical management of my hair. In altering its texture, I had made myself easier for *them* to manage. I had standardised my appearance and this seemed to have made everyone more comfortable.

When I thought back to those carefree days in Florence hurtling about in Marco's beloved *cinquecento*, the nostalgia physically hurt. Where was my '*cesto di capelli ricci*' now? I missed my 'basket of curls'. I was lost without them. I didn't like my slick new hair and I couldn't wait for the relaxer to grow out.

# CHAPTER FOURTEEN

# BLACK GIRLS
# DON'T SWIM

'Life's a funny old dog,' as Linda, my flatmate back in Florence, used to say. As a kid, I would have killed for the head of hair I had that day when I walked out of Raphael's salon in DC. It was soft and it was silky. It was easily brush-able and comb-able. It lay flush against my head and those teachers directing the Nativity play would have had no trouble with it at all. King Mel's crown would have slid onto that hair like a dream and he would have held his head high on any stage.

It felt like the ultimate irony. The only way I could put a positive spin on my relaxed hair was by viewing it through the invidious lens of my childhood. I now had the hair I had always dreamed of as a kid. I had hair that moved and fluttered in the breeze like everyone else's. Hair that didn't single me out as different. But as an adult, the reality had not lived up to my childhood fantasy. Every time I looked in the mirror, all I could see was a big mistake. It was a mistake I knew I was going to have to live with. At least for a while.

Back at the office, Myrna was my biggest cheerleader. When it came to my new hair, she was ready to wave coloured pom-poms and strut in front of a marching band. *That's* how good I looked. Now there was an evangelical edge to all her tips and pointers, as if I'd become a born-again convert and it was her job to keep the spiritual momentum going. I'd been saved, praise the Lord. I'd seen the error of my stubborn ways.

As my self-appointed hair adviser, Myrna informed me of the list of 'must-have' products I would now need to keep my relaxed hair looking good. She recommended all kinds of creams, oils, gels and conditioners and she placed special emphasis on *replenishing* natural oils, *strengthening and repairing* conditioners and moisturisers that not only *restored* moisture but *built up* the protein that had been *broken down* in the chemical process. Rather than reassuring me, I found this language troubling. It sounded as if it were putting a good face on defeat. Those words seemed to suggest that by relaxing my hair, I'd traded a strong, healthy head of hair for some delicate, feeble stuff that needed constant nursing like an invalid with a host of expensive medicines. Without knowing it, Myrna was fuelling my worst fear: that in relaxing my hair, I had signed it up for a lifetime of chemical dependency.

Now I hit the aisles in the drugstore like some twitchy junky looking for my next fix. My eyes raked the loaded shelves with a real sense of urgency. How to narrow things down from the profusion of choices? What did I need? Shine? Yes. Body? Yes. Softness? Yes. Strength? Yes. Moisture? Yes. Yes! *I needed all of it.* My hair had undergone shock therapy. It needed rehabilitating. It needed all the help it could get.

I remembered the early days in America, when I'd cruised the Black haircare aisles as if I were just taking in the sights, and they now seemed such innocent times. Back then, it had been no more than an intriguing pastime taking in the sheer amount and variety of products for Black hair. Now, my head reeling with Myrna's 'dos' and 'don'ts', I frantically scooped products off the shelves, stacking up my basket as if I were in a competitive trolley dash. When I unloaded my haul at the check-out, I barely flinched as the girl rang up the eye-watering total. For the moment, I'd let American Express take the hit and I would worry about the cost later.

In my bathroom, the products were mounting up. I was now doing regular drugstore sweeps looking for *the* most effective hair solutions. I began buying *Essence* and *Ebony* magazines just for the hair ads, so that I was constantly researching, refining and upgrading my stock. This one promised 'more control', but this one was 'ultra-hydrating'; then again here was another that claimed to offer a 'surplus of nourishment'. The products were taking over. Sometimes I had to hunt through a forest of tubs, bottles and aerosols just to find my toothpaste. My hair had become a round-the-clock project that needed more care than a hot-house orchid. I was going to be one of those women who had two overnight bags: one for my clothes and the other just for my hair products. With my natural hair out of commission until further notice, sustainability was now the name of the game.

When summer came around, the humid heat in DC was unbearable. Outside, the air lay in wait, ready to punch us with a hot, clammy fist. People dashed from the aircon of the office to the aircon of their cars in the parking lot as if trying to outrun the punishing heat. But on the bright side, it was pool-party season. A number of colleagues and friends in the office had their own pools and I soon got my first invite.

'*Girl*! Don't you even *think* about getting in the water with that hair of yours. You hear?' warned Myrna, my hair monitor.

I gave a grim chuckle.

'So what are you telling me? That I shouldn't go *swimming* at the *pool party*? That's ridiculous. Are you saying that girls don't go swimming once they've got their hair relaxed?'

'Not if they've got any sense they don't. Not unless you're going to smother it with a bucket-load of conditioner beforehand and even then... saltwater will dry it out, damage it, but I've gotta tell you, that *chlorine is a killer*.'

Myrna shook her head prophetically and cast me a doomed look.

Chlorine is a killer. This wasn't what I wanted to hear before my first pool party. What was the point of going at all if I couldn't swim? If I was too concerned about protecting my precious hair to even get into the water? I pictured myself sitting poolside, dry and demure, in the gorgeous electric-pink swimsuit I'd just bought for the occasion. I'd imagined cooling off with a few lengths in the pool before getting out to sip a glass of chilled wine. Was I supposed to sit there like some ridiculous poolside poser who was afraid of getting wet?

'If you *must* go in the water, you know you could always wear a swim cap,' suggested Myrna brightly.

I shut her down with a killing look. Swim cap? I don't think so. Not unless I was planning to be on the Olympic swimming team.

I mean, really? Who wore a swimming cap? It didn't so much cramp your style as annihilate it. I hadn't worn one of those appalling things since I'd learned to swim as a kid in the local swimming baths. We had no choice back then; if you were a girl, you couldn't get into the pool without one. Here was yet another flashback to the oppressive headgear I had endured as a kid.

I remembered the sweaty, damp stink of the girls' changing rooms and desperately trying to stuff the dense bulk of my hair into the clinging rubber as quickly as I could before anyone noticed I was struggling. The other girls slipped theirs on with little or no trouble, nonchalantly folding in the last stray wisps. We all hated those caps; the feel and the look of them, once on. Face it: no one ever looked good in a swimming cap, not even professional swimmers; not even Liz Taylor in her glammed-up version with its layers of petals that she had made fashionable for a while. No. A swimming cap would completely kill the effect of my hot-pink swimsuit, for which I'd even bought a coordinating towel. I was pool-ready and I planned to look stylish and cool – not like someone's mum. No. There was no question of a swimming cap, although I realised that with my 'new' hair, I wouldn't have to fight my way into one like the old days. But I was determined to go in the water just the same. Just watch me.

The pool party was out in the Maryland suburbs and it would be the perfect release from the sticky days in the city. So when Myrna told me she wasn't planning to go, I was surprised. Why miss the chance of a refreshing, cool dip in this airless heat? And it was in someone's private pool, with friends. But my surprise quickly turned to a sense of relief. I was secretly glad that Myrna was out of the picture and that I wouldn't be under her watchful eye at the party. Still, I was puzzled by what seemed like her lack of interest in the event.

'What? Don't you like swimming?' I asked her.

Myrna goggled at me as if I'd just asked her if she liked skydiving.

'Most Black folks don't swim,' she said curtly, as if it were something that my own common sense ought to tell me.

I shrugged at this, mystified. But by now, I'd got used to her abrupt manner. Myrna was known for shutting down a conversation when she was bored or couldn't be bothered. It was only later when I repeated her response to other Black friends that I discovered there was more to Myrna's remark than a simple brush-off. I learned that many Black Americans didn't swim; and there were strong historical reasons for this based more on access than ability. Back in the days of segregation, Black people were systematically denied access to municipal facilities such as pools, which were being built everywhere in the 1920s and 1930s. However prolific they were, these pools were usually located well outside of areas predominantly inhabited by

Black people, so that even after desegregation, they were not easily accessible to them. When Black individuals did try to access the pools, they were often met with resistance from white people, who found the idea of sharing the same water with them objectionable. At its worst, this sparked some violent racial confrontations where Black swimmers were beaten up and attacked. Desegregation in pools triggered what was known as 'white flight', which saw white people abandoning the public pools and retreating to country clubs or pools in more exclusive areas. Emancipation was all very well, but a swimming pool was considered too intimate a space for Black and white bodies to mingle. These old wounds cast a long shadow: 'Most Black folks don't swim' was a cultural hangover from the days of segregation; a charged memory that had stuck in the consciousness of Black people and in many cases had become a self-fulfilling prophecy.

But there were prevailing economic reasons at play too. As the public priority for municipal pools declined, one by one they began to close down without being replaced. Access to private pools, with their membership fees, were prohibitive for relatively poor people, especially in the inner cities, putting swimming further out of reach for many Black people. On the other hand, access to other sports such as athletics, basketball and football were all free within the school system and local communities. It's noticeable that even today swimming is one of the few sports in America where Black people are under-represented.

'We don't mind breaking a sweat, but we like to keep our feet dry,' chuckled one Black friend, summing it up.

So it turned out that Myrna's response to my breezy enquiry was loaded. It explained why many Black people in America have a contentious relationship with water and while plenty do swim, it's a recreational choice that still doesn't play a big part in Black American culture.

In my blundering ignorance, I had scratched at an old racial scar that still had consequences today. Now I was sorry that I'd been so offhand about Myrna's assertion, taking it to be no more than a conversational brush-off. Later, I explained to her that where I grew up in a small town in England, there were three rivers, and learning to swim was considered an essential life skill. I told her how once a week as eight-year-olds, my whole class were marched across town to the local swimming baths where we were put through our paces. An hour later, damp and bleary-eyed from the chlorine, we trooped back to school. Love it or hate it, we all had to get in the water.

At the party, it felt good in the pool; the water was so cool and silky against my skin after sitting outside where, even in the shade, the heat wrapped around us like cling film. But I was cautious to a fault. I didn't take a running dive or jump into the pool the way I would have liked, and the way I watched some of the others do. Instead, I lowered myself sedately into the water by way of the pool steps and once in, I confined myself to a feeble breaststroke, with my head well clear of the water. My doggy-paddle didn't feel much like swimming, but I knew that my usual power strokes from the shoulder with my face plunged in the pool were out of the question. Myrna wasn't there, but I could feel her shadow over my shoulder and I remembered her ominous warnings about chlorine being a killer.

I've always found swimming so relaxing, a complete release of body and mind. In Italy, I remembered the utter contentment of slipping into the warm, blue sparkle of the ocean under a blinding sun; pushing hard against the water with no sound but the gentle slap of waves around me. There was a sense of being suspended for a while in your own life. Nothing mattered but the shimmering blue landscape and being a part of it, moving in it.

Suddenly, men are shouting and women are shrieking; a water fight has broken out. It begins as a flirty splash-about in one corner of the pool – one of the guys flicking water at two of the women just to make them squeal. But the exuberance quickly spreads and others join in. Soon folks are thrashing water in all directions and men are wet-wrestling in an effort to dunk each other underwater.

Panicked, I haul myself out of the pool as if I've just heard gun shots in a bad neighbourhood. High and dry under a big umbrella, I sit pretty in pink, dabbing at my neck and arms with my designer towel while I watch the uproarious shenanigans from the side lines. Now a beach ball is flying back and forth across the pool and one shrill woman is trying to organise everyone into teams. She might as well save her breath, as the frolickers have no time for teams. It's a free-for-all as they abandon themselves to randomly batting the ball about with much yelping and splashing. This is exactly what a pool party should be: having a good time in the water while beating the pummelling heat. It all looks like terrific fun and I'd love to join in. But I'm a hostage to my own damn hair.

# CHAPTER FIFTEEN

# RESTORATION OF
# THE CROWN

How has it happened? Where has the time gone? When I first arrived in America with that three-month visa in my pocket, I could have no idea that I would still be here ten years later. Back then I'd told myself that I'd come for no more than a look-see. I'd give America the once-over, get it out of my system and get on with my life. Now, ten years older, I was thoroughly embedded in American life, with my own apartment, a car and a job, an ex-husband and a beautiful daughter. I had all the trappings of what Big Will would have called a *bougie* lifestyle.

In one of those old movies, you'd see a calendar flicking through the years in a few seconds of screen time to show the inexorable passing of time. In real life, I'd been around long enough to see three presidential seasons come and go and feel the political weather in Washington change with each. Carter, Reagan and then came Bush Sr. Most of my time in Washington sat squarely in the Ronald Reagan years of the '80s. Nearly always affable and jolly, the President seemed to have more of the 'aw shucks' air of a kindly uncle than the gravity of an international states-man. Nancy, his wife, ever chic in her couture two-pieces, somehow seemed more savvy than her husband. Like all First Ladies, Nancy Reagan was expected to publicly sup-port a cause close to her heart and she was famous for her 'Just Say No' campaign against the use of recreational drugs. Almost daily, there were pictures in the media of Nancy at a school or a youth centre surrounded by beam-ing kids who were ready to chant on cue: 'Just Say No'. It was short, simple and memorable; in just three syllables, it did everything a slogan should do.

It's not clear how successful the First Lady's campaign was in curbing drug use, but in any case, I decided to steal her slogan in my personal campaign against another kind of chemical dependency.

'Just Say No' *to hair relaxers*. Ignore the pressure. Resist temptation. Don't be influenced. Save yourself. Save your hair.

They told me it would take at least four months before I would begin to recognise my own hair again under the heavy-duty relaxer Raphael had applied. In fact, it took the best part of a year for it to grow out. I called it the 'wilderness year', when my hair was neither here nor there. Like a grudging stepmother, I tended to its needs perfunctorily, but I felt estranged from it. I wanted it gone. I didn't much care for that slick-haired imposter I saw every day in the mirror, but I tried to get on with her the best I could. It felt like I was serving time under that hair, but I made it clear that I didn't want any trouble from fellow inmates like Myrna. Once I'd seen out my sentence, I vowed to never go straight again.

I was almost afraid to tell Myrna that I'd found another stylist. Oddly, it felt as if I'd been sneaking around behind her back like a wayward spouse. Without any reference to her, my chief cultural officer, I'd gone ahead and taken my hair into my own hands. I'd gone over her head, so to speak. Fair to say I didn't expect a sympathetic hearing. In fact, I was ready for some stinging words meant to steer me back onto the right path. To my surprise, Myrna closed her eyes and shook her head with the saintly forbearance of a priest. She had done her best, but you can't save every drowning soul. Some of 'em will just slip right back into the water.

I'd often seen Jess at work as I walked past the big window of Sonny's, the Black hair salon near my apartment. It always seemed busy with people coming and going and each swing of the door delivered a short blast of jazz-funk into the street. The place intrigued me, although I always kept walking. Jess stood out not just because she was one of the palest Black women I'd ever seen but because she had hair just like mine. She wore it in a short, sculpted Afro and the only difference was that her hair was a natural fiery red. We'd caught each other's eye a few times over the top of a client's head she was working on and we exchanged shy smiles. I'd got a good feeling about her, a kind of yes-it's-my-natural-hair-and-I'm-not-afraid-to-wear-it vibe. It said something about her strength of character that she could work full-time in a Black hair salon in the '80s and not fall prey to the Way of the Relaxer. More than confidence, it was belief. It was a 'Just Say *Hell* No'. Our smile had seemed a tacit acknowledgement of this and it was exactly the reassurance I was looking for.

Even so, it was a while before things got any further than an encouraging smile. Given my sorry history when it came to hair salons, I was now like a dog with threshold fear. My first instinct was to dig in my heels. No. I won't go in. You can't make me. But with no one to yank my leash or drag me in with my paws scraping, getting up the nerve to go in and talk to Jess felt big.

This was not like Raphael's chintzy little place downtown. Sonny's was a huge barn-like salon throbbing to the funky rhythms of Fatback Band and Cameo; a space with the energy and feel of a disco that just happened to be a hair salon too. Under the bass groove of the music, the fusion of hairdryers with chatter and laughter rose up in a wall of noise. There was the usual set-up of chairs and mirrors down both sides of the long room where stylists worked with clients, but it wasn't all about hair. People stopped by the salon just to hang out and head-bounce to the funky groove for a while; they drifted in and out or lounged about on the two big black sofas at the entrance. Stylists, clients, friends, random boyfriends and the mailman swinging by for a coffee, at Sonny's there was a continuous flow of traffic. More like a community drop-in than a hair salon, the joint was always jumping.

Jess took me aside for a consultation and from the way she touched my hair when examining it, I knew I was in safe hands. Her fingers moved through it swiftly confident. I could tell she understood it; that she knew what she was dealing with. Unlike Raphael, who had handled my hair like alien growth that needed to be eradicated, Jess knew that my hair was not just raw material that was waiting to be processed. This stuff had its own natural energy that was not to be disrupted with artificial enhancers.

'It just needs a good cut and to be kept hydrated and healthy,' she diagnosed. 'I mean, why on earth would you want to mess with this? It's gorgeous just as it is.'

'Yes, it is,' I said simply, as if daring myself to say it out loud for the first time.

And it felt as if a truth had quietly settled between us that set us apart. This is who we are and this is the hair that we have. No need to drastically alter the DNA of it by attacking the hair shaft with harsh chemicals; no need to traumatise it. Let's work with it instead of against it. Let's see what it can do. In Jess, I knew I'd found a woman after my own hair.

It's all in the cut. It was that simple. This was Jess's mantra and it became mine too and one I've tried to live by ever since. Once the relaxer began to grow out, I put myself in Jess's hands. She had an eye for an impeccable cut, sometimes sculpting my hair into an angular boxy style that looked a little edgy, à la Grace Jones, and at other times contouring it softly to the natural shape of my head. Now, instead of hearing 'Where are you from?' all the time, it was 'Say, who does your hair?' People always complimented me on the cut and I gave out recommendations for Jess left and right.

Thanks to Jess, I got back the confidence in my natural curls and I even got used to the street-party atmosphere at Sonny's. I told myself it *was* a celebration. I was celebrating my natural hair, and this exuberant space, where even the mailman came in body-popping to Chaka Khan, was the right place to do it. It was a liberating space too. Across the music and through the soundtrack of dryers and gushing water, women were happy to yell their stories to each other. There were tales of cheating boyfriends, thankless husbands and the deadbeat ex who was still trying to borrow cash.

'Lord save us from the triflin' ways of men,' cried one woman with a head full of tightly packed rollers, lifting her eyes to the heavens.

To this there was an immediate response of 'Amen' and 'I heard *that*!' so that for a moment we might easily have swapped the swivel chairs of the salon for church pews.

I always felt too timid and too much of an outsider to 'get down with the girls' in these lively exchanges. I was also self-conscious about exposing the stiffness of my British consonants among so much free-flowing and colourful talk. Instead, I listened, the way I used to back in the language labs at university with the earphones clamped on. Like tuning into a foreign language, I rode out the rhythms of the talk all around me, thrilled by its energy and vitality. As the salon became a noisy confessional, I listened in, attuning my ear like a jazz lover to the different tempo and phrasing.

In Jess, I'd found not just someone who can do wonders with my hair but someone with a temperament that suits me. While I hear other stylists gabbing long and loud about everything from their relationships to make-up to TV soaps, Jess is that rare bird: she is a stylist of few words. When she's working on my hair, neither of us feels the need to feed each other vacuous details about our lives and loves. Against the pumping background of Rick James's 'Super Freak', Jess works calmly and methodically as she cuts. There's a zen-like serenity about her, which I absorb. At times, despite the surrounding clamour, I often find myself drifting into a meditative state. So when she leans into my ear one day and indicates to me in the mirror the woman sitting behind us, I know she's got something worth saying.

I check out the woman who is at the early stage of having her hair relaxed while she's flicking through a copy of *Jet* magazine. The stylist has on her protective gloves and is clarting the thick cream relaxer over the woman's hair in gluey, white streaks, pulling it evenly right through from the roots to the tips. Its familiar scent of bad eggs and ammonia permeates the salon all day long, but now Jess and I get a strong, nose-wrinkling whiff of it. I have to clamp my lips together and adopt a shallow breathing pattern.

'There's goes another one,' Jess whispers fiercely into my ear. 'Another one killing her hair on an instalment plan.'

Standing in the power of our natural curls, Jess and I know better. We share a complicit smile in the mirror, as if between us we possess the secret wisdom of the ages.

# CHAPTER SIXTEEN

# MOTHER LOVE

'Oh yeah. No question. It's almost definitely gonna be a boy.'

Standing back from me in the corridor where she'd stopped to assess my growing baby bump, my co-worker was adamant. I watched her look over my belly, appraising its size, shape and position with the eye of a professional clinician.

'I can tell by the way you're carrying it,' she said, backing up her conviction with knowing nods. 'Believe me, I carried my first in just the same way. He was low-slung too, just like that.'

'Gherkins and smoked salmon, eh? I guess you're having a boy,' another smirked confidently as I unpacked my lunchtime bagel.

While yet another baby-fancier crooned, 'There's no

mistaking it. You've got that "baby-boy glow" about you! What you gonna call him?'

I smiled and accepted the well-wishing and wisdom of older and more experienced women. This wasn't just guesswork or intuition; these women knew stuff. Like the ancient sibyls and soothsayers, they saw signs in everything: how I walked, what I ate, my changing looks. All these things foretold only one thing: I was expecting a boy. It was like experiencing the Annunciation on repeat; and just like the Virgin Mary's 'according to thy word' response, I accepted their forecasts with serene inevitability. Why argue with that kind of hard-core belief? After all, what did I know about babies? This was my first time around the block and I was discovering that women, even women you barely know, feel they have some kind of stake in your pregnancy. It didn't bother me. I was fit and healthy and I was having a boy. That was all I needed to know.

In the face of overwhelming opinion, I didn't dare mention to anyone that I'd originally set my heart on a girl and that I was struggling to come up with a likely name for the little fella. But even though a little boy felt like unknown territory, I was excited to meet him. I was sure that my Josh or Ben or Marvin in the making would be a wunderkind of some description – and whether that was as a fireman or a financial whizz on Wall Street, I didn't much mind. What's more, there was a lot to be said in favour of a baby boy. In my mind, boys were easier in so many ways.

You had only to see all the fussy frills and flounces in the baby clothes designed for girls. There was something about the fluffy pinks and lavenders, with their flowers, hearts and butterflies that I found oddly repellent. Why must they all be so – well – *girly* and so cloyingly cute? When it came to baby girls, it seemed impossible to find simple, unadorned clothes in everyday colours; clothes that weren't trying to tug at your heart strings like a basket of puppies. *So precious! So adorable!*

On the other hand, you didn't have to pretty boys up. No need to dress them up like some kind of life-size doll. You knew where you were with boys' clothes. They were simpler and so much more practical in their earthy greys, greens, browns and, of course, blues. And as long as you avoided the superheroes, I found that I didn't mind the odd train or boat motif on their little outfits.

And then there was the inescapable matter of hair.

During my time in America, I was good friends with a Black couple who were parents to three little girls. This meant they had to partition a good part of every weekend to managing the girls' hair. With a whole kit of oils, moisturisers, specialist combs and hair accessories, they sat for hours dividing the girls' hair into sections, parting, combing, plaiting and braiding it before securing it into place with colourful barrettes and hair toggles. Both mother and father took responsibility for the girls' haircare and it was built into the weekend routine. Along with the supermarket run, cooking, cleaning, church, kids' parties and family time, there was also hair maintenance to be factored in. The girls sat at their parents' knees reading a book or watching TV or sometimes just bowing their heads in relaxed submission as their parents went to work on their scalps while chatting over their heads with family and friends. With grandma occasionally acting as backup for haircare, you could be sure that at the beginning of each week, all three girls had a head of gleaming, neatly braided hair that was nothing short of a labour of patience and love. Those little girls grew up in the full knowledge that their natural hair was worth the trouble and that it mattered to their vision of themselves in the world.

While I'd had my own hair braided and plaited as an adult, it was a skill I had never learned myself, and given my own childhood hair struggles, I felt ill-prepared for this kind of parental responsibility. I knew only too well how instilling a culture of good haircare as early as possible was key to developing self-esteem and a robust sense of identity in Black girls.

But boys were different. You couldn't go wrong hair-wise with a boy. All you had to do was cut it and go; maybe with a little more finesse than Mary, my foster mother, had done all those years ago, but it was a straightforward process that consumed little time or emotional energy. Later, they could have all kinds of cool cuts, but as kids, Black boys' hair was low maintenance compared with the girls. Having a little boy meant I would dodge that bullet. I would be able to keep my pitiful lack of hair smarts in hiding. I was off the hook.

'It's a beautiful baby girl!' said the obstetrician from behind the screen. Numbed from the waist down by the epidural shot I'd been given earlier, they had placed the C-section screen across my chest, so that while I could still feel all the pressure of pushing and pulling, I was spared the sight of the gory tug of war taking place below my navel.

A girl? I was genuinely stunned. I had been carrying this 'baby boy' narrative around since the early days of my pregnancy. The runes had been cast. The oracles had spoken, and as far as I was concerned, I had signed up for a boy. All those women had been so emphatic. They had left no room for doubt. How could they all be wrong? It was their cast-iron predictions that had flipped the switch in my brain to 'boy' mode and there it had stuck; their certainty that had me sizing up fire engines and dump trucks at Toys 'R' Us and imagining all the blue ribbons on my congratulatory cards and flowers. Just weeks before this, friends and work colleagues had thrown me a baby shower. There had been a big cake and baby gifts galore and women insisting that we were celebrating the imminent arrival of my baby boy.

It's a girl? My first thought was: *Could you check again, please?* Maybe that vital part of male anatomy was hiding somewhere in the folds of the furled little creature I could now see the nurses were busy examining and wiping down. I sat up on my elbows, craning for a better view. A girl? Are you sure?

I was thrilled with my little girl, Phoebe, from the moment they settled the soft weight of her in my arms. But all too soon she was whisked away to the hospital nursery while I recovered from the protracted labour that had unexpectedly ended up in the operating theatre. The next day, when the nurse brought her into the room I shared with another new mother, we compared babies. I managed to find some kind words to say about her bundle of joy, but it wasn't easy. Truth be told, there was no comparison between my perfect little pearl-faced, almond-eyed beauty and the crinkly faced goblin-child she was cradling. My baby girl shone like a jewel and I was bedazzled by everything about her. What really fascinated me was her head of dark, dead straight hair. It was the softest, silkiest jet-black hair you could imagine. There was not so much as a hint of curl or kink in it. I combed it with trembling fingertips, lost in wonder at her tiny, sleepy face and suddenly overawed by the depth of meaning in the word 'mother'.

If I'd known anything at all about the development of Black babies (and why on earth would I?), I would have known that her hair wouldn't stay that way for long. After a few weeks, her pearly-pale complexion got darker and as the months went on, those silky, straight strands of hair began to curl, softly at first into a fluffy kind of fuzz, then tighter and ever tighter until it became hair that was just like mine.

My friends taught me the importance of massaging her hair and scalp with moisturisers and oils from the beginning and finger-combing it all the way through. This was something she seemed to love as a baby, sending her into what looked like a blissful-baby trance; but as her hair became thicker and the texture slowly began to change, there came a point when I couldn't run my fingers through it so easily and I was forced to use a hair pick or a wide-toothed comb.

And so began the weekly regimen of intensive haircare. The sheer amount and density of Afro hair can be overwhelming at first, but as the famous TV chef says when it's time to taste his latest dish, you just have to 'get in amongst it'. I visualised what I had seen my friends doing with their three girls. I began by dividing the damp hair into quadrants, sectioning them off with big claw combs so that I could concentrate on a quarter of her head at a time. I detangled as much as I could with my fingers and then carefully used a wide-tooth comb. Next, I stretched out the curls to their full length from root to tip, moisturising as I went, before combing it through in sections and then plaiting it up. I did the best I could, but I was acutely aware that my hands had no history to fall back on and my fingers had no memory. The casual agility and speed that I'd admired in my friends did not come naturally to me. I have small, rather delicate hands; ideal hands for the job, you might think. But somehow my fingers always felt thick and clumsy as I worked them through Phoebe's hair. I knew that there was no way I could pull off any of the intricate hairdos that I'd seen on lots of other little Black girls; all I could do was draw the dense mass of her combed-out hair up into two fluffy pom-poms or (when she would let me) into a series of lumpy, uneven plaits. I was disappointed in myself. Here was my chance to sow the seeds that would help her blossom into a confident young woman and I was letting her down. What kind of mother was I if I couldn't provide my daughter with a positive sense of her physical self in the world? Was I failing in the fundamentals of motherhood?

As Phoebe got older, I was dismayed that our hair time together didn't get any easier. Far from the mother–daughter bonding experience I'd hoped for, it actually became an area of real contention between us. Despite my best efforts, history seemed to be repeating itself. Had I not learned anything from my own sorry experience? Why was I handling this so badly? After all, I could see myself in this little girl in a way that I had never had a chance to see myself in anyone before. We looked like each other and she was the first blood relative I had ever really known. I wanted her to feel good about herself in a way that I never had been able to as a kid. And yet I would find myself bristling with impatience as she wriggled and squirmed away from the comb, no matter how gently I tried to handle her hair. I tried to distract her with TV and her favourite pop music, but the comb-out was always fraught with tears and recriminations; I was hurting her. That was enough. Can we stop now? Please? These hair sessions often had to be completed in stages with regular breaks that allowed us both to calm down and de-stress. Like prize fighters between rounds, we would retreat into our separate corners and try to regain some strength.

A grown woman now with her own children, Phoebe still remembers those comb-outs as the 'Sunday evening nightmare' that was guaranteed to plunge us both into the doldrums and put a damper on the last precious hours of the weekend together.

'I was always so tender-headed,' she says in retrospect, 'but maybe it was because my scalp had never had a regular workout with all that tight braiding that most Black girls go through from an early age. I always felt as if my head was being vandalised.'

Vandalised! So much for what I believed was my compassionate approach. Vandalised. It's a tough word and yet it struck an all-too familiar note. I began to wonder if my own early trauma was quite literally at the root of my inability to deal properly with my own daughter's haircare. In painful flashbacks, I could still feel Mary's brushes and combs tearing into my hair and unknowingly yanking it out at the roots; the bristles hopelessly snagged in the tight trap of curls so that sometimes a brush or a comb had to be cut out together with the clumps of hair. I relived the sore scalp, the stress headache, the guilt and the humiliation. Could it be that, subconsciously, I was passing the memory of my own physical and emotional suffering on to my daughter? That my miserable experience as a child had made me too squeamish to deal with the same problem with my own daughter? In fact, I was so afraid of hurting her, so over-sensitised to *her* pain that I would back off at her slightest wince or twitch of discomfort. I lacked confidence with her hair and she sensed it. Like invisible radio waves, I was transmitting my own anxiety, and this certainly didn't help. Far from deepening our mother–daughter bond, the weekly comb-out was driving a wedge between us. But it had to be done. Without it, her hair would become hopelessly matted into impenetrable clumps where trapped dust welded with her hair's natural oils. Without the comb-out, her hair would become the same dry, knotty mess that I had had to endure myself as a child.

This weekly hair wrangle was wearing us both down, so when she was ten years old, I took Phoebe to a professional Black hairdresser for a consultation. But when the stylist recommended a 'texturising' treatment, she saw my face drop. I already knew that this involved a relaxer, albeit a much milder version than I had experienced myself, but a chemically driven process nonetheless. Seeing my expression, the stylist was quick to reassure me that the texturiser would not straighten her hair but merely loosen up her tight curls and make it *so much* easier to manage. It was completely safe, she went on breezily, and it would make all the difference in the world. I was still shaking my head when the stylist decided to override my dubious looks and appeal directly to my daughter.

'Then you'll be able to do your own hair, won't you? Just think how fun that will be!'

This stylist, I realised, had quickly understood the broken dynamics in the mother–daughter relationship before her and like a therapist she knew exactly where to apply the pressure. My happiness depended on my daughter's happiness and her happiness depended on her hair, the root cause of concern, if you will. The stylist made it clear that with just the right amount of alchemy, she could fix it – all of it. Not just the hair, but she could repair the mother–daughter rift that the hair had created; a rift she had detected in the cloud of anxiety hanging over all three of us. I could see that in my daughter's eyes, the stylist had become the fairy godmother of the piece while I had been cast as the glowering villain. What's more, the stylist had trumped my doubts by throwing in the 'F' word. Up until now, *fun* had never played a part in our hair sessions together. Until now, the words 'hair' and 'fun' had never worked well in the same sentence. Fun, the 'F bomb', might just be the game changer.

With her head inclined to one side, my daughter gave me that look of silent pleading that parents struggle to resist the world over. I could feel my metaphorical arm being twisted all the way up my back.

Reader, I texturised her. I know. It was chemicals and she was still just a kid. But I couldn't seem to fix it myself. The 'Sunday evening nightmare' was turning into the 'Sunday evening stand-off', as she often refused to let me launch a thorough comb-through and I knew that her hair was not getting the attention it needed. I'll confess that to avoid conflict, I sometimes bunched it all back into a hair net and secured the net in place with a hair band. This arrangement simply hid the problem and was no solution. I knew it would soon be out of control and I would have to resort to the 'crisis crop'.

So, yes. I opted for the chemical cop-out, but it allowed Phoebe to manage her hair for the first time. She still had the density of her curls, but they were softer and silkier and she could now brush it, comb it and style it herself with ease. In terms of her self-esteem and independence, this was a huge change. All I wanted was for her to feel happier about her hair. And she was happier. She was in charge now and it took the pressure off the weekends for both of us.

As the Black mother of a Black child, I had a distinct sense of personal failure in having resorted to a chemical process for my daughter's hair. I was a fraud of a mother who had found a questionable quick fix to make up for my parental shortcomings. There was no excuse. Sure, I was a single mother working full-time, but I, of all people, ought to have learned or made it my business to learn the proper hair skills. I should have made time for it. I felt as if I had given myself a dishonourable discharge, but my guilt was counterbalanced by my daughter's new-found confidence and positive attitude to her hair. What's more, it had broken the cycle of conflict that had threatened to overshadow our otherwise happy relationship. We still

had the usual arguments about pocket money, clothes and
sleepovers; none of that changed. But when it came to her
hair, as the stylist-cum-fairy-godmother had predicted, it
made all the difference in the world.

## CHAPTER SEVENTEEN

# OTHER-MOTHER LOVE

Mary, my foster mother, had already been dead for a couple of years by the time Phoebe was born in America, but I couldn't help thinking about the dilemma she had faced all those years ago. What chance did she stand of coping with this 'other' kind of hair in the depths of rural Yorkshire? How could she have known its super-resistant properties to ordinary brushes and combs and the damage these everyday grooming tools would cause to the natural growth of Black hair? How could she have known that it needed regular moisturising treatments to prevent it becoming too dry and brittle and that a comb-out should only be attempted on damp hair and with specialist combs? And how, for heaven's sake, had an unworldly, working-class, white woman of middle years in 1950s small-town Yorkshire ended up fostering a couple of mixed-race kids in the first place?

Although Mary was only in her early forties when she began fostering, she always seemed terrifically old to us kids. While I know that most parents seem that way to their kids, Mary felt more like a foster granny than a foster mum. She was not just old-fashioned in her shapeless cardigans and eternal pinafores but *old-looking* in that worn-down-by-life way of so many working-class women of the time.

Going into service with the local gentry when she was fourteen years old, Mary barely had a youth when she married at twenty. She had been a housewife bringing up two of her own children during the '40s when, like everyone else, she had suffered the disruptions and deprivations that wartime inflicted on family life. Used to rationing during, and for many years after, the war, Mary was of the generation who believed that leaving even a scrap of food on your plate was a shameful affront to human decency.

The truth is that, back then, women like Mary *were* old in their forties. Life was an unrelenting daily grind where they washed, cooked, baked, cleaned, knitted and sewed clothes for their families. All this, long before the convenience of the automatic washing machine and spin dryer, the food processors and the powerful vacuum cleaners we take for granted today. Few working-class families had cars, so the landscape of most housewives was inevitably a limited one. Except for the occasional trip to the shops, they were

chained to their domestic environment and the needs
of family. The responsibilities of childcare and the unre-
lieved drudgery of laborious household chores was their
entire world. However clever and resourceful these women
might be, few of them had much formal education. If they
read anything, it was at best a copy of *Woman's Weekly* that
was passed from neighbour to neighbour, although this
implied a leisure that was rare, and they were more likely
to read something of immediate use such as the *Be-Ro
Home Recipes* book or a knitting pattern. There were few
diversions from home life and that was just as well, because there was very little money for it. The cinema or the
'pictures' was for the young folks; kids went to the Saturday matinees and couples went in the evenings to snog
and squeeze in the dark. Eating out was almost unheard
of, unless it was at a wedding or a funeral, and was deemed
an obscene extravagance that made no kind of sense. Why
pay good money to go out and eat food made by strangers
– and in public! As for travel, if you were lucky enough
to have a car, there might be the odd trip out into the
countryside or in summer to the seaside (with a packed
lunch eaten roadside on the way) and just enough money
for an ice cream and a bag of cockles on the sea front. In
most families, the entire running of the household usually
stood or fell on the husband's weekly pay packet. Many
working-class families were strapped for cash to the point

of strangulation and making ends meet was an anxious weekly struggle.

Jack, our foster father, was a semi-skilled mechanic who worked for the local bus company while moonlighting occasionally for a haulier firm that belonged to one of his mates. He also had a sideline as a cobbler, a skill he had picked up in wartime and for which he turned the garden shed into his workshop. He was a keen amateur photographer who developed his own films by blacking out the kitchen window with army blankets; it's thanks to him that I have so many random, grainy pictures from childhood. Meanwhile, as well as doing stints as an unpaid neighbourhood childminder, Mary took orders for sewing and knitting. I can still see her hunched over three needles, following the complex patterns for the fashionable Fair Isle sweaters that were always in demand. This, I suppose, was her leisure time.

In a working-class household in the '50s and '60s with only one slim pay packet, it seemed that you had to have a sideline to survive. This was the generation that had navigated the privations of wartime Britain, so they were experts when it came to developing sidelines. They had had to 'make do and mend' for so long that it had become second nature to adapt whatever life skills they had to their advantage. What they might have lacked in education, they made up for with hard work and ingenuity. If you wanted additional income, you had to have another string to your bow and a little hustle to go along with it.

Mary, I believe, had always liked children, but by the time I arrived on the scene at three years old, their son was an independent young man in his twenties. As for their daughter, Mary's world had been shattered years earlier when, one day, at nine years old, she had been knocked down and killed by an army lorry. The poor girl had just been running a routine errand and she never returned. A picture of the dead girl hung on the wall in the sitting room, but her name was rarely spoken and only then in the hushed, reverential tones of a hopeless prayer. This trauma had left Mary with a sense of guilt and loss that haunted her for the rest of her life. In later years, she hinted to me that it had ended what little sexual intimacy she had not so much enjoyed as endured with Jack. Like so many of her generation and class of women, sex was just another chore. You had to put up with it for the possibility of babies and then for the sake of keeping the men happy, but on the whole, it was an inconvenient, distasteful business and the sooner it was over the better. There was no doubt that the suppressed grief for the death of this child had seriously disrupted the husband-and-wife dynamics in the marriage; but like so many other bereaved post-war couples, they made the best of things and soldiered on.

So how had it happened? How had the fate of not

one but two unwanted mixed-race children collided with
Mary's world in the rural white heartlands of Yorkshire?
That she was fond of children is clear, but another mixed-
race friend fostered in similar circumstances at the time
believes it was flagging family economics that played the
biggest part in the appeal of becoming a foster carer back
in the '50s. It wasn't big money, it's true, but those few extra
pounds a week would definitely ease the pressure on that
pay packet. It's easy to imagine how some women might
have reasoned: why not make a little money for something
I've been doing for years with neither pay nor recognition?
Besides, foster care was a charitable act; you were helping a
vulnerable child at a crucial stage in their life. And anyway,
how much trouble could two fuzzy-haired little coloured
girls be? Fostering allowed you to work from home and
required no other skills than showing a willingness to be
a good mother to an otherwise homeless child. It wasn't
easy money by any means, but it was extra money that
with thrifty management could make a significant difference to a low-income family. The extra cash may even
have given some women a little financial independence
from their husbands.

'Some women took in washing, others took in children,' said someone of their own unhappy experience as a
foster child in that era. But despite the obvious economic
advantages of fostering, I think that would be unfair in

Mary's case. With the sudden death of her only daughter all those years ago, taking care of other people's kids may have helped to alleviate the still-painful loss, and given a new stimulus to her life and a wider outlook. In its advertisements of the time, Barnardo's was seeking 'Christian homes' and 'kind families'. There were pre-placement assessments and home inspections and once a child was placed in a foster home, there was ongoing monitoring from Barnardo's social workers who documented the behaviour and progress of each child in detailed records throughout their care. Still, it's hard not to feel that there was something random about our placement and that we were dropped like dark little aliens among the unsuspecting earthlings of rural North Yorkshire. More likely, I suspect, any family anywhere in the country that was willing to foster Black children back then would have been embraced with open arms.

That Mary and Jack had absolutely no sense of racial awareness should come as no surprise to anyone, since few people did back in the '50s and especially outside of the urban areas. While Leeds with its growing Black community was only twenty-five miles away, it was so far from the reality of our lives that it might as well have been Narnia under the wintery spell of the White Witch. At the time, being able to 'overlook' our colour was probably the strongest thing in Mary and Jack's favour as ideal foster parents, and once that hurdle was surmounted, any issues that might arise from our different ethnicity seem barely to have been taken into consideration. In fact, our glaring physical difference to everyone around us was the elephant in the room that was quietly, if pointedly, ignored. To all intents and purposes, we were all colour-blind and Black was the colour that dare not speak its name. When racism raised its head outside of the home, as it inevitably and often did, we were not encouraged to ever make a fuss about it or to use it in evidence against anyone or anything. People stared; carry on and ignore them. Kids called us names; keep walking and ignore them. Resilience was the name of the game and we quickly learned the rules. As for our problematic hair, even if Mary had had the first idea of how to manage it, who had time for all that palaver, all that faffing about with specialist combs and whatnot? Of course, kids should look neat and tidy (and we always did), but nobody could be expected to pay that kind of attention to a child's personal grooming. It made no sense. No wonder she reached in exasperation for the quick fix of the scissors.

'Racial literacy is defined as an understanding and appreciation of both racial and cultural differences, as well as the realities of racism and discrimination,' explains one study on the challenges of transracial fostering and adoption. There's a lot of talk about it now. Today, adoption and fostering services fully recognise some of the issues for white families parenting Black children. They emphasise the importance of seeking out opportunities that expose the Black child to their own culture, through community, music, art and literature in order to develop a sense of identity and belonging.

And some of the modern agencies have taken the issue of Black haircare fully on board, offering workshops and videos on Black haircare aimed at educating white parents in how to take care of their child's hair. They emphasise the different approach that is needed when managing Black haircare, advising against 'over-washing', which strips natural oils from the scalp, leaving hair dry, brittle and frizzy, and warning never to comb hair out when dry. Some even suggest recipes for home-made hair moisturisers using almond or olive oil with rosemary and lavender. They also remind parents that, just like white hair, all Black hair is not the same and they encourage speaking to Black hair professionals for individual advice on texture and care. Dedicating time to looking after a Black child's hair appropriately is now recognised as an important part of parental responsibility for white carers. It's not just hair but identity – and Black Hair Matters.

That my foster mother's heart was in the right place,

there can be no doubt, and to be fair, there was at least one attempt on her part at what I'm sure she believed was cultural relevance.

One Christmas when I was four or maybe five, I got a gift of two brightly illustrated board books: *Epaminondas and his Mammy's Umbrella* and *Epaminondas Helps in the Garden*. The name of this character was fascinating enough, even though I could barely pronounce it; somehow it sounded grandiose and nonsensical at the same time. But looking at the pictures in the book, I didn't like the look of the title character. Epaminondas was a scrawny little Black boy with goggling eyes, rubbery red lips and nappy hair. This dim-witted piccaninny was prone to every kind of mishap, as he was batted back and forth like a ping-pong ball between his mammy and his auntie on a series of errands. These two women who wore elaborate kerchiefs on their heads, the likes of which I had never seen on any Yorkshire woman, were coal-black just like Epaminondas and with the same stereotypical thick lips and bulging eyes. But it wasn't just the illustrations that confused me; the language had an unfamiliar ring to my ear too. The two women regularly exclaimed at the child's ineptitude with phrases such as 'My laws a-massy!' and 'My gracious sakes alive!', and his mammy always scolded him with the same curious expression: 'You ain't got the sense you was born with.' Who talks this way, I wondered?

Was it some kind of make-believe talk? Why did it all sound so strange?

I didn't know what to make of this skinny and stupid boy or the adults who didn't seem to understand that he was some kind of simpleton and not to be trusted with the most straightforward job. While I knew that I was meant to see humour in the stories and illustrations, it seemed to me that this child's misadventures with lettuces, eggs and umbrellas were more to be pitied than laughed at, and everything about these little books quietly troubled me.

Mary knew I loved books, and in choosing *Epaminondas*, I realised that she believed she had hit just the right note. This would connect me with a character with whom she thought I could easily identify. Only I didn't look or behave anything like Epaminondas. I wasn't coal-black, I didn't have those comical distorted features and I'd heard plenty of people say (not without some surprise, I'll admit) that I was pretty bright for my age. I felt hurt and yet guilty and ungrateful at the same time.

The books were written by Constance Egan, an English author, and illustrated by A. E. Kennedy, and they were published in England in the late '50s. Egan, it turns out, had re-told the stories from folk tales originally published by the American author Sara Cone Bryant in 1911. Bryant had, in her turn, poached the stories from traditional oral folk tales from the southern states of America. It's quite disconcerting when you see some of the original American illustrations to Bryant's book. Epaminondas has the face and slouching demeanour of a sly rascal; his features are animalesque in what was then, no doubt, the stereotype in the US of the lazy and slow-witted Sambo. I didn't know it at the time, but the funny language I encountered was a caricature of everyday Black folks in the southern states of America and if Mary had read them, which I doubt she had time for, she would have been as baffled as I was when, after another botched errand, Epaminondas's mammy warned him: 'Now I ain't gwine tell you any more ways to bring truck home.'

I looked at Epaminondas's nappy knots and I remember thinking: *Do people think of me like that? Is this the way I look to others? Does everyone think I'm some simple, pop-eyed little darkie?* Even at five years old, I could detect the adult mockery behind the illustrations and language of the hapless go-between and the two Black mammies, and it disturbed me in a way I couldn't properly understand at the time. When many years later I discovered that the real Epaminondas had been a Greek general and statesman in the fourth century BC, the irony was complete. In comparing the luckless little negro with an outstanding military strategist from the ancient world, Bryant had had the last laugh.

All I knew was that I didn't want any of my friends

to read or even see the books. I could almost hear them snickering at the words and pictures and saying Black people not only look funny but they talk funny and are pretty stupid into the bargain. It would feel as if *I* was the joke. They would look at my dark skin and dry tufts of hair and think: *We have our Alice in Wonderland and our Peter Pan, but* these *are your people.* So I suppose with Epaminondas, Mary was trying to cater to some kind of racial awareness. As for me, I knew better than to tell her how much that little Black boy alarmed me and that I was much more at home among the woodland creatures in *The Wind in the Willows.*

I have friends who became registered foster carers some years ago after undergoing a rigorous assessment process. In proving their eligibility for the roles, they were subject to every kind of scrutiny as the authorities took a deep dive into all aspects of their lives, past, present and future. Income, financial records, employment records all went under the microscope and their marital relationship and relationships with family and friends were investigated together with a close look at how they had parented their own children. People from within their immediate family circle and others outside were called to give testimony as to their fitness to foster. References were requested from near and far, including certificates of good conduct from foreign law enforcement agencies accounting for their previous residence abroad. Health and safety checks were made of the house and they were told of required modifications and adjustments. There was training both online and offline to be completed, with courses on child development, child trauma and building resilience in children, as well as a familiarity with the Children's Act of 1989. Once approved as foster carers, they were required to document and evidence everything about the child in their care, keeping extensive notes for their frequent contacts and meetings with link workers, social workers and the Looked-After Children worker. It's a lot. But this process tries to ensure that today no one undertakes foster care who is not assessed as wholly committed to the welfare and well-being of children and that this is at the forefront of their interest in becoming foster carers. It's an exhaustive vetting process, but fostering agencies will leave no stone unturned in their efforts to recruit carers with the right level of dedication and understanding.

Recent changes in the political and social climate, particularly since the Black Lives Matter movement, have seen social services, local authorities and fostering agencies taking an even closer look at how we look after Black children in care. They recognise the importance in trying to place Black children with Black foster carers who will make them feel more at home while providing them with a cultural mirror. But the reality is that agencies up and down the country struggle to recruit Black carers, so the racial imbalance in foster care is hard to ignore. Statistics tell us that there are far more Black children in need of foster care than there are Black families in the fostering pool, where there is already an overall shortage. So while agencies stress the importance in matching children with families who look like them, understand their cultural background and can maintain the connection with their heritage, in fact the odds are much lower in placing Black children in foster care than white children and even less of placing them with Black carers. So the call-out continues for Black carers to take up the fostering baton from all agencies. 'Children in care need more people from our community,' said an experienced Black foster parent of thirty years standing in a recent article in *The Voice*, the British national African-Caribbean newspaper. The carer called for more Black people to take up fostering with the prospect of changing a child's life for the better. She said that she believed a deterrent to many Black families was the level of scrutiny and sharing of information about their personal lives that fostering would entail, but she went on to remind readers that this was because the child's welfare and safety are paramount. Other Black carers agree that the fostering process needs to be demystified to attract the right people from the Black communities. The UK's leading fostering charity, the Fostering Network, recently published an article exploring the under-representation of Black carers. Some of the Black carers believed 'there is too much red tape which puts people off. Simplify the process and change the style of recruiting, make it more real, more fun.' Until there is a levelling up of Black carers, all agencies now agree that foster carers need to be able to tap into the help and support from people who are of the same ethnicity of the young person in their care, and that supervising social workers and fostering team managers need to facilitate this. Encouraging and strengthening these connections is now considered an essential element in a Black child's foster care.

Of course, it's a notion that would have been absurd back in my era of being a foster child in the '50s and '60s. Many newly arrived Black families, mostly from the Caribbean, were struggling with their own identity issues as they tried to get a foot on the job and housing ladders in what they were quickly discovering was a racially illiterate and often hostile Britain. These people had their own challenges to deal with as they tried to integrate and they had often left their own children in the care of extended families back in the Caribbean until they were more settled in Britain. But I do sometimes wonder, if I'd been brought up within or around a Black community, would I have liked myself any better as a kid and a young person?

Would I have been better at being me? It's nice to think I might have been less confused and more confident about my looks and my identity. And I wonder, with the support of a Black community around me, if I would have brought that sense of cultural confidence to motherhood and been able to pass it on to my daughter, especially in how she saw herself reflected through the challenging texture of her hair.

It makes me smile to think that, had I grown up in the digital age, I would have been able to connect with some of that identity online just like I see my teenage granddaughter, Chloe, doing. A mixed-race girl in a pre-dominantly white community, she's learned everything she needs to know about her hair and its unique prop-erties on YouTube, TikTok and specialised podcasts. It's all out there now for everyone. Her entire hair education has been learned from mini-screen masterclasses that she can play over and over as often as she likes. It's like learning herself online. There she can see girls with the same kind of hair not struggling but happily manipulating their hair into complex patterns and creative styles. After her early unhappiness in trying to manage its volume and tough texture, she and her hair are now 'besties', as she's fully aware of its tremendous versatility. She braids it, she weaves it and is constantly surprising us by creating new styles and looks. While the virtual world is no substitute for real friends and experiences, there is no doubt that it can be a powerful support and a learning tool for those who feel themselves disconnected from their cultural heritage.

# CHAPTER EIGHTEEN

# ONE DAY IN RIO

They say the best time to come up here is at sunset. That's when this staggering view is steeped in a mystical golden glow, and off in the distance, on top of Corcovado, *Christ the Redeemer* seems to be blessing the whole jaw-dropping panorama. From the city of Rio and the green mountain-scape beyond, your eyes sweep along the white beaches of Copacabana and Ipanema to the marina where sailboats flicker like white moths on blue-blue water. I'm on the observation deck on top of Sugarloaf Mountain in Rio de Janeiro, and it doesn't seem real. It's as if I'm caught up in some vast dreamscape and I'm likely to wake up from it soon. I have to stop taking pictures and just give myself a moment *to be* in the picture; to be present and alive to this swooning sense of wonder. I need to absorb it, breathe it, believe it.

When I came back to the UK after ten years in the

United States, I felt as if I was good for nothing. I kept sending out my CV and getting nowhere. I couldn't understand it. I'd worked in a major European embassy in Washington DC where my job in a busy press office had covered daily contacts with the federal government and the American and international press, as well as translating and speechwriting for the ambassador. As diplomatic support, I'd covered everything from disasters such as the devastating earthquake in southern Italy in 1980 to the opening of prestigious international exhibitions in Washington's National Gallery of Art. I'd 'made my bones' with the Italians, and when a small, hand-picked group of embassy staff accompanied the Italian ambassador and senior diplomats to the G7 Summit in Williamsburg, Virginia, you can bet I was among them.

Back in England, I'd imagined that with my solid work experience in the US, I would breeze into a job of my choosing in international relations or press and PR. And perhaps I might have done in London, but as a single mother returning to the UK after years overseas, I chose to come back to Yorkshire where I'd grown up, and where I wanted Phoebe, my small daughter, to grow up too. Yet it felt as if local recruiters didn't get me, and my glowing CV was proving more of a hindrance than an advantage. It didn't impress, it merely confused prospective employers. I'd worked in some fancy embassy abroad? Well, so what? And it wasn't even a *British* embassy. What was that about? I knew that to many outsiders, embassies often seem to have an intimidating mystique. With all that impenetrable security, who really knew what went on inside their walls? Still, I was mystified. There seemed to be few 'takers' willing to consider my employability.

When I did get to interviews, I knew that I would have to manage the surprise factor. Whoa! She's Black! They never saw that coming. Nothing on my CV had prepared them for that. I could have given them a hint, at least. I would have to slide into my 'I-may-be-Black-but-I-come-in-peace' mode to put everyone at their ease before the interview even began. So besides my unconventional look, no one seemed able to transpose the skill set I'd developed in Washington to an everyday job in provincial England. I was a square peg in a world full of round holes. I might be interesting, but was I relevant?

At first, the idea of a job in the civil service didn't entice me in the least. Before university, I'd done a spell in a bleak unemployment benefit office in Leeds and it had crushed my youthful spirit. But, older and wiser now, when I took a job as a regional government information officer, I knew there would be variety and plenty of scope to get out and about in the region. One of the first clients I worked with was the Foreign and Commonwealth Office (FCO) and its overseas visitors section. The visitors were foreign VIPs from all over the world invited by the FCO to meet with government departments and agencies in London and beyond. My job was to design programmes that were tailored to their interests and expertise in the Yorkshire and Humber region. Accompanying foreign ministers and delegations into prisons, universities, hospitals, local industry and once, even down a working coal mine, it was a chance to relearn the region I'd grown up in; while the visitors from Mongolia to New Zealand gave me a welcome waft of the wider world that I'd been missing now that I was back in Yorkshire. But it was only when I began promoting government export services that I got a chance to travel overseas myself.

In joining overseas trade missions, I was able to capture the 'export journey' of the participating Yorkshire companies as it was happening and file the reports back to local newspapers for publication in their business sections. Working alongside the trade officers in the British embassies and consulates overseas felt like familiar turf, and when I wasn't out at meetings with the companies, I spent a lot of time at desks in overseas posts, knocking out copy for the papers. I did this in Milan, Prague, Barcelona, New York and, in 2004, in São Paulo, Brazil.

Flying over the São Paulo skyline, you get your first glimpse of the gigantic metropolis that is home to more than 12 million inhabitants. This landscape of never-ending skyscrapers, which is the financial capital of Brazil and the foremost industrial centre in Latin America, makes the New York skyline look like a village. As the plane bounced onto the runway, I realised that my general knowledge of Brazil was nothing more than a list of popular clichés: coffee, carnival, samba, football.

The trade visits seldom give you a true sense of the country. The time constraints on the few days' programme mean there's little opportunity for sightseeing, socialising or interacting with the local community. At best, you get a taster, and if you're lucky, a feel for the country. Brazil, I quickly learned, was no country for vegetarians. Meat is big in Brazil, and you will often go to restaurants where you are served course after course of sizzling beef cuts until you can eat no more. I preferred the informal *por quilo* buffets. Here, once you've chosen your food, it's then weighed and you pay for the weight, per kilo, of whatever food you have on your plate.

I also learned that almost 50 per cent of the population of Brazil is of African ancestry; transatlantic slavery having brought more Africans to Brazil than any other country. Here they worked on the sugar, coffee and rubber plantations and later, when gold and diamonds were discovered, in the mines. It's fair to say that African slavery in Brazil helped fund Portugal's expansion across the world. One thing I noticed straight away in Brazil was how well

I blended in with a lot of the population in the same way as my blonde, blue-eyed pal Linda had merged with the locals in Scandinavia. Looking around me in São Paulo, I saw many people who looked like me with the same complexion and texture of kinky hair. Like me, almost half of the population is of African-European descent (*pardo*) in Brazil, though some areas have a higher density of white people than others. In fact, I looked so natural that people would often mistake me for a native Brazilian and begin speaking to me in Portuguese. '*Não, não é possível,*' they would exclaim disbelievingly when I claimed to be British like the rest of the group I was with. I found that my Italian helped. It was close enough to Portuguese to be understood, and it meant that I, in turn, understood more of this soft and inviting language when I listened closely.

'You need to go to Rio to meet with the oil and gas trade officer over there. We're looking at a proposed visit next year,' my boss back in Leeds instructed me with a matter-of-fact email.

Rio! Really? Rio had never been on the cards for this trip and I wasn't even sure where it was on the map in relation to São Paulo. But I was surprised to discover that Rio was just an hour away by plane and that the commute between the two biggest cities in the country was considered quite routine. Even so, the idea of taking a day trip to Rio sounded deliciously urbane. And so, like Fred

Astaire and Ginger Rogers in the glamorous old movie, I found myself 'Flying Down to Rio' for the day. It was May, so much too late for any carnival action, but I was still hoping to get a flavour of the vibrant buzz of this iconic city.

The meeting at the consulate in Rio took only a couple of hours, so there was time for a little sightseeing before my plane back to São Paulo that evening. I decided to scale the famous Sugarloaf Mountain: a monolithic 400-metre-high slab of granite rising straight out of the sea above the harbour. Taking an organised climb to the summit was an option that I quickly rejected in favour of the thrill of the cable car that I could see dangling dizzily over the bay.

At the Sugarloaf summit, people exclaimed, gasped and 'Wowed' at the view, swivelling their cameras in all directions. At first, I got caught up in the tourist fever with everyone else. I began snapping pictures in a frenzy like a journalist in a war zone – fast, one after another, from every possible angle. I ran around the observation deck as if I was working against the clock on a deadline. But I soon felt as if the camera was getting between me and the moment. I just wanted to fill up on the sumptuous view. I let my eyes drift dreamily across the city, sandwiched between the forested-green mountains and the sparkling blue of the South Atlantic. I was wide-eyed and wordless. I've never much liked that overused expression the 'wow factor', but it was hard to stop myself from mouthing the word, if only silently to myself. It was while I was in this state of enchantment that I noticed a woman further along the viewing platform who, instead of gaping at the marvellous view, appeared to be gaping at me. I glanced at her and looked politely away, but then found I had to look again. It was like looking at my twin sister. We laughed as we both recognised ourselves in each other; the same hair, the same skin colour, the same facial features right down to the freckles across our nose. I'd never met my lookalike before and the magnetic force between us was too powerful.

Felicia didn't believe I was British either, but she spoke excellent English and told me she was a radiographer from Recife in the north of Brazil and she was in Rio attending a healthcare conference. We had coffee together in the little cafe and talked about the difference between being Black in Brazil and Black in Britain. Felicia was shocked to know that I'd lived out my Black experience in the UK almost entirely within white spaces, something that would have been hard to do in Recife, she said, where almost half the population were mixed-race, like us.

'But you didn't straighten your hair and that's a good thing?' she said, as we admired each other's upstanding and abundant hair.

The history of my hair was too long a story to share with Felicia, who told me that Afro-Brazilian women struggled with the concept of keeping their hair natural in a culture that still prized Eurocentric ideals of beauty despite the high proportion of people of African descent in the population. Then she told me a true story.

Tiririca was a circus clown and comedian turned popular singer, and back in 1996 he wrote and released a recording of a 'humorous' song that had caused a cultural storm in Brazil. In the lyrics of his song entitled *'Veja os Cabelos Dela'* ('Look at Her Hair'), he compared an Afro-Brazilian women's hair to a scouring pad for cleaning pots and noted other derogatory things about her, including her bad smell. There was such a public outcry against the song that the record was seized from stores and Sony music, the distributors, were consequently sued for racism. While Tiririca was prohibited from performing the song in public, he protested that it was meant to be a joke, passing it off as nothing more than a bit of harmless fun, in the way that we often hear racial slurs in the UK shrugged off as a 'bit of banter'. But there was a feeling among Afro-Brazilians that the disparaging words of the song reinforced culturally sanctioned beliefs that demonstrated the accepted notion of white superiority. By giving people permission to laugh at and denigrate the racial attributes

of Black women, said Felicia, the song was a telling por-
trayal of the image of Black women in popular Brazilian
culture.

It was a shocking tale; another old and oft-told story
of how our natural hair is weaponised against us to re-
inforce a sense of inferiority and shame. The 'scouring pad'
reference reminded me all too painfully of the 'wire wool'
comparison that the Yorkshire hausfraus made about my
own hair as a child; a remark that still had the power to
make me flinch. Like Tiririca, they had seen Black hair as
something harsh and abrasive and ultimately laughable.

Felicia and I talked about hair as a marker of racial and
social identity in Brazil and beyond. And how for many
Afro-Brazilian women, 'hair that swung' or 'loose hair' was
the ideal look that they wanted to achieve. While more
Black women were choosing to stay natural in Brazil,
Felicia believed that unlike in the '70s, when it had been
more about racial consciousness – in Brazil too, they had
been greatly influenced by Black American activism and
the Angela Davis look – now it was more about self-
acceptance, racial confidence and an expression of who
they were as women.

'I believe our hair has enormous energy, don't you?' said
Felicia. 'We should let it speak its natural language.'

We took the cable car together, gorging on our last

bird's-eye view of Rio as we glided back to ground level, where Felicia helped me get a taxi back to the airport.

'*Adeus, minha irmã*,' she called from the other side of the taxi window. Goodbye, my sister.

On the flight back to São Paulo, I reflected that I had only spent six hours in Rio but it had not disappointed. I'd experienced something of the city's enduring fascination and I'd met Felicia, who gave me a keyhole glimpse into a more intimate picture of the country and what life might be like for someone who looked like me in Brazil.

Felicia had once again highlighted the central role that hair plays for many Black women in processing their identity and how quickly and glibly the rest of the world can undermine it just for the sake of a good laugh. I was hurt and angry for Felicia and every Afro-Brazilian woman who had suffered the public mockery of 'Look at Her Hair'. That we lived in a world where the most personal parts of our identity were considered ideal material for toxic 'comedy' no longer surprised me, but it was still galling.

Now I was going back to write a story about a Yorkshire company hoping to export its healthcare training services to Brazil. A piece I had promised for the next day to the business editor for the *Yorkshire Evening Post*. The company had had some promising meetings in São Paulo and it would be a good, upbeat report about a local business making headway in a huge foreign market. Even so, I knew my heart wasn't in it. I wished that I was writing a story about Felicia and all the women like us.

'Our hair has enormous energy,' Felicia said, and I knew she was right. If only I could convert that energy into real-life stories that spoke its truth of resilience, resistance and powers of transformation. Stories that might seed change and maybe shift perceptions of how we see ourselves and how we are seen.

# CHAPTER NINETEEN

# ROOTS OF INSPIRATION

I'd like to go back to India, to see more and to feel more. I didn't recognise it at the time, but I now know that India was the start of something.

Up in the pure mountain breezes of Dharamshala, I'd envied the centred stillness of the Buddhist monks floating about with their enigmatic, dreamy smiles. I'd longed for a transformative experience that would give me something of their spiritual calm. But it was not to be. I blamed myself. I hadn't allowed myself to be open to it. Enlightenment had been within my grasp, but I had let it slip away from me. In the midst of so much serenity, my mind was in turmoil as I relived past hurts. So instead of coming back to England mellow and chilled out as I had imagined, India had unsettled me. Along with the sublime, I'd seen appalling scenes of hopeless poverty and hard-scrabble lives that were hard to reconcile with our habits of wealth and waste. And on a personal level, the taunting kids had stirred up difficult memories. Back in England, I felt vaguely cheated of the spiritual journey that I had been promising myself. I'd expected a new version of me on my return with a complete shift in perspective. Yet here I was, the same old me; I was back at my desk again writing a press notice to deadline while choking back a tuna sandwich.

But as the dust settled, I could feel something beginning to crystalise. Maybe enlightenment is not a sudden, blissful transformation; not a goal in itself. It's a gradual and ongoing process of becoming and discovering potential. Maybe enlightenment is a work in progress. Slowly, I began to sense the stirrings of something new within myself.

I knew that what had bothered me in India with those pestering kids went deeper than embarrassment or vexation. It had dug up forgotten fragments of my childhood excavating long-buried anxieties and shame. Washed back onto the shores of my childhood, I reconnected with the uncertain, confused little girl in the home-made golly suit with the ragged mop of hair; the kid who's trying to dredge up a smile that just won't surface. The kid who later believed if she could just unkink her hair, it would miraculously unkink all the difficulties in her life. It was only after India that I was ready to revisit her again in all her uncertainty and confusion. And I knew that I wanted to celebrate her with her own story. The kind of story I know that she would have loved to have read and treasured.

Thanks to my advanced reading age and a natural propensity to daydream, I never lacked imagination as a kid. But nothing I ever read, saw or heard led me to believe that my hair was a thing of beauty. It was not until people like Linda, Mamie and Marco, the Hair Whisperers, laid loving hands on it that I began to understand its extraordinary power and possibilities. When I think of myself as a fretful nine-year-old literally tearing out my own hair in the toilets, I wonder: what if I'd been free to imagine a different sort of crown; a natural, grow-your-own crown like the one Mamie had fashioned out of my own hair that time; a crown for all seasons? The memory of wearing that natural-grown crown had stayed with me as well as how good it had made me feel.

I'd always wanted to reimagine a Rapunzel-type story for the kinky-haired, frizzy-haired girls like me; a story where hair would be our triumph and not our tribulation. So I wrote a children's book that reflected its outstanding adaptability. Just like King Mel, in *Princess Katrina and the Hair Charmer*, Katrina battles to keep her crown in place. She knows that she has the 'wrong hair' for a princess because she's seen the pictures of princesses in the storybooks. With their long, flowing hair, they don't look anything like her. She tries to keep her spirits up by staying busy, but she is beginning to doubt that she really is a proper princess. It takes the magical Hair Charmer Zuri to convince Katrina that her hair is 'just crackling with joy' and that it is an adventure in itself; that in its strength and complex texture lies its incredible versatility.

'Because your hair is so *strong* and *so full of itself,* Miss Princess, it can do the most amazing things.'

My thoughts were to create a fairy tale that wasn't about spells and magic but that suggested the practical yet amazing possibilities of Black hair. My 'Rapunzel' would not be redeemed by attracting the love of others but by discovering her love for herself and her natural attributes; a story not about getting the prince and living happily ever after but about getting her self-esteem and learning to live happy now. In writing *Princess Katrina*, I wanted to create an uplifting, inspiring tale about the power and the glory of our natural hair for all the kids, like me, who had only ever felt defeated by it.

*Princess Katrina* was one of the first children's books of its kind to celebrate the fun and creativity in the distinctive texture of Afro hair. Hair was the hero that came to the rescue. Hair was the energy of the story. In transforming the hurts of the past into a positive message for the future, the story reached out to little Black and mixed-race girls everywhere. But it was only when I began to tour schools with my book that I realised that what was a story of affirmation for many Black and mixed-race kids was nothing short of a revelation for many white kids, who were alerted to the unique properties of this kind of hair for the first time. Hearing these kids say, 'Black hair is so cool' and 'I wish my hair would do that' was the best kind of feedback.

'Go on. Guess. Guess which one is me.'

I've always wanted to play that game. You know the one where you produce one of your old school class photos and challenge friends to pick you out from among the rows of youthful faces? But in my case, there would be no point. There's just me: the one Black face. I'm the dark blot on the white landscape. Me, and my big head of springy hair disrupting the visual uniformity of the picture. I hated being different back then, and in those tortured sessions with my spiky rollers, I was doing everything I could to stretch my hair straight. I believed that straight, or at least *straighter*, hair would downplay my difference.

'That's better, Tina!' gushed the gym teacher one day with a big cheerleader's grin.

I hadn't had time to comb my hair into shape before school that day, and out of frustration I had tied its bulk back into a thick wad behind my head. Not so much a bun as a wedge.

'That's so much tidier, isn't it?' said the teacher, still smiling hugely.

Received and understood. *Flatten it down, tie it back, tame that stuff*, was the message behind the cheesy smile. Meanwhile, I ran track, was in the hockey team and I was fairly popular, but I knew that, unlike my girlfriends, I was never in the running for a real boyfriend. I had the usual big crushes, of course, on this boy or that, and some close 'boy friendships', but they never developed into anything more. I didn't blame them. It was the '60s in rural North Yorkshire and it was a conservative grammar school. You would have needed a tough skin to form an attachment with the only coloured girl in the school. You might never live it down. Years later at school reunions, you'd always be *that guy*; the one who had the hots for the Black girl when there were pretty white girls a-plenty to choose from. *What was that about? No, really. What?*

Although I did have a boyfriend for a while outside of school, who was a few years older and already out in the working world. With his shoulder-length hair and long Afghan coat, this lad had all the trappings of a hippy, which was a brave look in a small town like ours. I'll never know if it was because he was into Jimi Hendrix that he liked the look of me or if we were drawn to each other because of our unorthodox looks and an abundance of hair. I wasn't a Hendrix fan myself, but I remember the boyfriend buying me a record of Jimmy Cliff's 'Wild World', a song I love to this day. Decades later, I ran into him and he made a point of telling me how much ribbing he'd got from his workmates back then for being with the Black Girl. 'What's up? Couldn't you find yourself a white one?' they had jibed. By then, I had a university degree, had lived and worked in Italy and America and back in the UK had become a respectable civil servant with a young daughter and my own home. While I knew that the 'ex' had said it in nothing more than a spirit of shared nostalgia, it surprised me how hard that was to hear all those years later. I saw myself again at sixteen looking all wrong but doing my damnedest to fit in. This one boy had made me feel 'normal' for a while. I had a boyfriend like the others. Somebody liked me too and didn't mind showing it. To discover, all these years later, that his mates thought I was a joke was still hurtful. It felt like a long-delayed aftershock from my teenage years; a time when I knew I was working hard to play down my difference and believed I was doing a good job of it.

These days, instead of trying to live it down, I try my best to live up to my hair. When the mood takes me, I love to draw attention to it, glamming it up with flashy accessories that show off its volume and strength. But mostly, it seems to speak for itself. Whether I like it or not, my hair draws people. Like the time I was slumped on a bus, tired at the end of the working day. When a young man got on and sat next to me despite there being plenty of empty seats available, I was quietly alarmed. Maybe he actually knew me and I'd forgotten who he was? Maybe he knew my daughter, Phoebe? Maybe he was some kind of pervert who liked molesting older women on public transport? But no.

'I simply had to sit next to the woman with such wicked hair,' he said with a cheeky grin.

Or the waiter at a restaurant in Rome who hovered about our table as if we looked like big tippers. It was only when serving dessert that he confessed that he hadn't been able to take his eyes off my hair.

'It's like a wonderful halo!' he said with an unexpected tenderness when he served us coffee.

Mindful of the danger of accepting any male attention in Italy, I thanked him politely, and I thought: *Yes, I'll take that.* As we watched the sun sink behind us at the Colosseum, I gloried in the moment, which was probably the closest I'd ever come to feeling saintly.

Wicked and wonderful, what more can you ask? From compliments to come-ons, my hair often upstages me, and unlike that time at the Taj Mahal many years ago, nowadays I'm happy to embrace it.

'My hair isn't performing tonight,' I told a friend as I checked the mirror on the way out to the theatre.

Because I really believe that it has its own personality and moods. Sometimes it's stubborn and wilful. On those days, it will do what I want but only up to a point and no further. Just don't push it, it warns me. Another day, it's compliant and playful, ready to please. And then there are times when it's crackling with confidence and wants to go full jazz-hands show-time. I cannot keep it down.

'*Ogni riccio un capriccio*,' say the Italians. Every curl a whim. And none more whimsical than our natural Afro curls. As a kid, I agonised about all the things this hair couldn't do, but now I continue to be amazed by all the things it can.

Wicked and wonderful it may be, but the more I think about it, the more I appreciate its natural properties.

Afro hair holds its own. It can be your secret pocket: its density and strong texture means it can hold and lock small objects in its tight network of curls. I remember storing things in it at school like a spare pen or pencil or a stick of chewing gum; an object I would often forget and only rediscover when I went to bed and my head hit the pillow. For a while as a teenager, I fancied myself as a smoker, and my hair was the perfect place to stow away a contraband ciggy. *I'll smoke that later*, I'd think as I threaded it into the complex tangle of my curls, confident that it wouldn't fall out and it would stay completely hidden. It was a secret just between me and my hair.

Afro hair is its own art form. Whether in the complex geometrical patterns of cornrows or in twists, locs, knots or dozens of fine braids, it can express our moods, feelings and personalities. Some Black female artists have found that their hair has become a powerful communication tool that reaches beyond beauty. By exploiting the properties of its unique strength and pliability, they have been inspired to create dynamic sculptures out of the hair on their head. This can be seen in the creations of artists like Laetitia Ky, a fashion designer from the Ivory Coast. After seeing pictures of pre-colonial African women and the obvious pride and poise with which they carried their extraordinary natural hairstyles, she was intrigued to see what her own hair could do. At first, Laetitia began diligently crafting her hair into playful shapes, but she soon realised how she could advocate for change with her hair sculptures by making arresting visual statements about female equality and education.

Our natural hair is a continual inspiration for art projects in all mediums, from painting and printing to photography and sculpture. Black conceptual artist Hank Willis Thomas created a giant Afro-pick sculpture that recently toured major US cities. *All Power to All People* is a steel sculpture that stands two storeys high and carries a powerful message in all the public spaces it has occupied. The simple, everyday object, symbolising collective identity, racial representation and Black beauty, makes a silent but monumental statement. A nine-foot version of the sculpture could be seen in a recent outdoor exhibition in London's Regent's Park, where its uncompromising message still had the power to stop people in their tracks.

Afro hair is like horticulture: just ask Jess, my old stylist back in DC. To create the defined geometric shapes for box and buzz cuts, Afro hair requires the precise eye and the close-clipping skills of a small-scale topiary artist. This makes sense since our hair often has the same compact density as the tight foliage of evergreens such as box and yew shrubs, lending itself to the same artistic approach to creative shaping and design.

Afro hair is topography and code: runaway slaves are said to have used intricate cornrow patterns to hide maps from slave owners and their would-be captors. By literally encoding the lay of the land into their hair, they could form secret escape plans and communicate messages to facilitate them. In other words, hair could quite literally map the road to freedom. By the same token, distinctive hair patterns could be used to communicate almost anything. In an environment where behaviour and communication between slaves were ruthlessly monitored, hair could be used as code. A language they alone could read.

Afro hair continues to give rise to music, poetry and prose: from medieval madrigals, literature and modern verse to rap music and R&B pop, our hair naturally weaves its way into words and songs that express our vision of ourselves and challenges the way others may see us. Unlike her sister Beyoncé, Solange has publicly revelled in choosing to wear her hair naturally. In the lyrics of her song 'Don't Touch My Hair', she reveals that her natural hair is about so much more than how she looks. It expresses how she feels, too. The soulful song needs no explanation to most Black women, who immediately understand the vulnerability and defensiveness the singer is expressing about her natural hair.

It's practical, it's artistic, it's soulful, it's secretive, it's poetic, it's musical, it's historical, it's political; our natural hair carries with it a multiplicity of messages and arouses so many deep feelings. Shapeshifting, outstanding and headstrong, it has the ability to morph and adapt, which is what Black people have been doing since for ever. And like us, it has a coiled energy that doesn't take life lying down.

As we move away from the notion that being beautiful means chasing after white standards of beauty, we are standing up for our Afro hair the way it has always stood up for us. However dark our skin and however kinky our hair, we are beginning to understand that we are enough.

When I think back to my 'wilderness year' with relaxed hair, it was as if I were in mourning for something vital that had been lost. Not just a sense of definition but of natural balance. I was out of kilter with myself and felt incomplete. My natural hair had its own protective force field. It was how I knew myself best and without it I'd lost my identity; an identity I'd had to build in isolation from my own lost history but which I knew bound me to generations of Black women before me. What's more, in losing my natural hair, I seemed to lose not only my confidence but some of my complexity. I couldn't get over the sense that my chemically altered follicles had wiped out some of my character.

Safe to say that whatever we Black women feel about our natural hair, it touches a deep vein of sensibility. It invites us to examine the gap between who we honestly are and who the world tells us we ought to be or *be like*. And it's not easy, because today we are besieged. How do we hear our own voice in the relentless yammer of online opinions? How do we identify ourselves in the flashing images we're exposed to every minute of the day on social media and TV? Where is the silence and space to reassess?

It sometimes feels as if tapping into our true selves and recognising our own worth requires a devout meditative exercise such as those practised by the Buddhist monks in the prayerful foothills of northern India.

'Happiness will never come to those who fail to appreciate what they already have,' said the Lord Buddha.

# CHAPTER TWENTY

# THE POWER AND THE GLORY

*'And even the very hairs of your head are all numbered'*
MATTHEW 10:30

O nce upon a time in a village somewhere in the Africa of our imaginations, a company of women sits under the familiar shade of an old acacia tree. Finally, they are released from the day's back-breaking labours. Like beasts of burden, they've carried calabashes of water up from the river; they've pounded the maize or groundnuts until their bodies ache; they've tended mewling babies and settled the disputes of quarrelling children; they've built fires and prepared and cooked food for their men and families. Now, as the sun slides below the dark canopy of the forest and fireflies begin to sparkle in the dusk, women and girls gather together laughing and talking at ease. With an unspoken intimacy, many of them settle themselves at the feet or between the knees of others who with hand-crafted combs begin working on their heads; their fingers darting like lightning through the only hair they have ever known. Hair whose strong and complex texture reassures them as they work, with a tender sense of acceptance and belonging. They smooth it with palm oil to nourish the scalp and roots, giving it a sheen and making it more flexible to work with. Then they carefully comb and part it into sections of geometric precision. The women have an instinctive feeling for this hair; nimble fingers know their way through the complex network of roots and tangled curls and they skilfully control its strength and energy. They know just how much tension to apply as they braid it like strong thread into fantastic patterns against the scalp. These are the patterns of their lives, their hardships, their hopes and their joys. This is them, themselves, uninhibited and free from the judgement of men. In this relaxing and restorative time of the day, they unravel their stories, sing their songs and open their hearts to each other, and the hair itself is part of the structured weave of their daily lives, a vital part of their intimacy and fellowship.

In these unguarded hours, when wisdom smooths the daily wrinkles of worry and gives way to gossip and laughter, the women invest each other with a sense of pride and belonging as their fingers manipulate ingenious land-scapes and architecture out of their hair. They appreciate it for what it is, prizing the elasticity and toughness of its texture that allows them to show their dexterity and creativity. It holds messages too. In designs that express everything from tribal allegiance and marital status to se-duction and *joie de vivre*, this hair has a voice and it speaks for itself.

All this was in the twilight of the 'beforetime'. It was before these women knew that history had other plans for them. It was before their past was stolen and before the bitter journey to hostile shores where lives of unimagina-ble hardship, degradation and loss awaited them.

In her fascinating investigation into Black hair, *Don't Touch My Hair*, social historian Emma Dabiri says that early European travellers to Africa spoke positively about the texture of Black African hair, marvelling at its capac-ity to form intricate weaves and ornate styles never seen before. But all that changed when colonialism and slavery took hold and the balance firmly tipped in favour of the white European norm. This became the gold standard for everything, including hair. It now suited the narrative of the day to view African people as no longer fully human – they didn't even have proper hair, for heaven's sake, *they had wool* like livestock. Once African people became a commodity, African-textured hair was seen as inferior and associated with a kind of non-humanity and 'otherness'. Our hair was seen as more trouble than it was worth and for those who survived the hellish voyage to the Americas, many would be shorn like sheep on arrival.

It's these powerful and painful narratives that have left us with the damaging legacy that haunts us today and that so often blights our relationship with our natural-born hair. Like Old Testament prophecies echoing down through the ages, the judgements of people who saw us as nothing more than commercial property still weigh heavy. These negative perceptions are at the root of so much that has been written, said, thought and felt about these mar-vellous, convoluted strands that grow out of our head and are – as someone once murmured to me under the Italian stars – 'so alive' and 'so beautiful'. History never goes away, and this hair is loaded with it.

'I can barely remember what my original hair looks like,' I heard one Black woman say in Sonny's salon. 'I've spent so much time and energy hiding it and putting it out of sight.'

'As a kid, I was brought up to believe straighter is always better and the straightening comb was always right there, hot and ready in our house,' another commented.

'Yeah, you've gotta stay on it,' vocalised a third woman. 'Nothing worse than having two inches of naps and six inches of straight hair.'

I used to hear snatches of conversation like this all the time in Sonny's salon. Women's voices rising above the din as they interrogated the ambivalent relationship they had with their hair. Like those distant village gatherings, the salons are the safe spaces where Black women can talk most freely about their struggles and anxieties with their natural hair. I discovered that some feared being 'caught out' with their natural kinks, as if they had been exposed in public in their underwear. They wouldn't be seen dead without a good weave or relaxed hair and some even prided themselves on never letting husbands and partners see their hair in its natural state. Since childhood, they had been locked into a cycle of weaves or relaxing and it was the only way they knew. They believed that their natural hair made them appear 'too Black' or untidy or not attractive or feminine enough. They felt not just a desire but an obligation to normalise their hair, as if they had a duty to protect not only the white world they moved in but also themselves from the complexity of their difference.

These are deep, dark waters and whichever route we choose on our hair voyage, it's not plain sailing, because there's a lot more to it than navigating tricky hair texture. Every day we steer around the politics of race, gender and sexuality as well as charting a course through the trends of fashion and culture. The fact is that it's a rough old sea out there for we Black girls and our hair, and few of us are experienced pilots. Each of us is mapping our way with our personal compass, trusting instincts and belief.

But sometimes society's pressure can feel stronger than the weight of our own instincts. Like a lot of women of colour, I feel like I've spent the best part of my life being told how I ought to feel about my hair. It's laughable, it's weird, it's cool, it's sublime, it's groovy, it's messy, it's passé, it's political, it's a 'statement'.

Years later, with the party vibe of Sonny's salon in DC long behind me, I found myself in a salon in Leeds sitting next to a woman who was having her hair relaxed while her small daughter looked on wistfully from a nearby chair. Except for the fact that her hair was neatly braided, I saw myself in that little girl with her longing eyes, searching for some beauty in herself. You could tell she couldn't wait for her turn to come. She was desperate to get that slick, glossy hair like her mum; she couldn't wait for a stylist to slather that magic potion on her own hair and transform her into the kink-free fairy-tale princess she deserved to be. Mum was an office manager, and when I asked her what lay behind her choice to relax her hair, she answered without hesitation: 'I don't feel people take me as seriously in business when my hair's natural. With my hair relaxed, I feel more professional. More confident. Plus, let's face it, I'm easier on the eye. I'm less of a visual and cultural challenge.'

There are still many Black women with the same conviction. Their hair in its natural state is seen as an obstacle to their professional and social lives. It's unpresentable, unattractive and unstylish. It may be expensive to keep up, but however low your income may be, it's a matter of self-image and personal pride. As to the risks from the cocktail of chemicals in the relaxers, unless you were one of the unlucky ones, you tried not to dwell on the reports of scalp burns, hair loss, respiratory problems and headaches. You needed straighter, more mainstream hair, and relaxers did the job. And you can't put a price on looking good, can you?

But how much difference does it really make? Does straightening our natural hair actually give us an edge in professional and social opportunities? Are we 'less of a visual and cultural challenge' when we straighten it out? Well, I've only to remember how hard Myrna lobbied for me to relax my hair, while hinting darkly about the negative consequences to my work prospects by staying natural. And I also remember noticing that my straightened hair seemed to make other people feel more at ease.

Well, that was all back in the '80s, you say. But it's interesting to see that Michelle Obama, wife of the former US President, only feels able to wear her hair in natural braids now that she is no longer in the international spotlight. Even standing at the side of her Black, natural-haired husband, there was never any question of her daring to wear a natural style as the First Lady. America, and probably the rest of the world, would have weighed in with their disapproval. Even as late as 2017, keeping her hair natural was a political statement that she, along with her two young daughters, knew she couldn't afford to make. During one of her recent book tours, she was quizzed about what seemed a radical change of style after her carefully coiffed days as First Lady. Michelle believed that during her husband's presidency, Americans 'weren't ready' to deal with her natural hair. It would have become an 'issue' that would have over-shadowed her husband's political goals. Her thinking, she tells us, was: 'Let me keep my hair straight and let's get healthcare passed.'

Michelle, who as a successful Black American female lawyer fighting for racial justice had her own impressive story to tell, had no doubt hoped that her book tour would offer opportunities to discuss some of her work, projects and beliefs; she probably hadn't expected to get sidetracked by talking about her hairstyle choices. But it clearly shows that how a Black woman chooses to wear her hair is still up for public debate and can quickly upstage any conversation, not to mention international politics.

In the past twenty-five years, the internet has put a world of information at our fingertips and we are all more attuned to the environment and personal health issues.

Informed Black consumers are now confidently interrogating the cosmetic industry about their care and concern for Black women's health in the products they are marketing. In the case of chemical relaxers, their concerns now appear to be well founded, as mounting evidence from recent landmark studies indicate that the risks of some relaxers may be much more than skin deep. The studies have found alarming correlations in the sustained use of relaxers and some serious long-term health issues for Black women.

What has come to light through the research is that there is a strong correlation between women who have regularly used lye-based (sodium hydroxide) relaxers over the years and an increased risk of breast cancer. Sustained use of these relaxers is also associated with double the risk of uterine cancer for Black women. As the evidence stacks up indicating the long-term health risks, Black women worldwide are relinquishing their dependence on relaxers and recalibrating their relationship with their natural hair.

We've now entered a new and interesting time of influencers and 'wokeness', which is shifting the cultural dial around the policing of natural Black hair. In 2019, California became the first state to ban discrimination against Black people based on natural hair by passing the CROWN Act (Creating a Respectful and Open World for Natural Hair) and the state of New York quickly followed. Today, the CROWN Act is law in twenty-five states across America and a bill has been passed in the US House of Representatives that 'prohibits discrimination based on a person's hair texture or hairstyle if that style or texture is commonly associated with a particular race or national origin'. The bill is still waiting for national approval by the US Senate.

Here in the UK, we are only just catching up. Slowly. When, in 2016, a fourteen-year-old girl was repeatedly sent home from school because her natural hair was deemed 'too big', the case became a national sensation and a catalyst for the equality watchdog the Equality and Human Rights Commission (EHRC) to issue guidance to schools stating that students should not be stopped from wearing their natural hair in schools. While it's good to know that there is guidance in place for the educators, it doesn't stop kids with natural hair from being regularly bullied by their peers.

'Nice face, shame about the hair,' recalls the mixed-race daughter of a friend of mine when looking back on her experience as a fifteen-year-old in an all-white secondary school. The flip remark was made by a boy she admits to quite fancying at the time and she remembers how it left her feeling shame-faced and worthless. Years later, as a successful fashion consultant, that comment along with other hair-shaming incidents in school still rankles, but like a lot of us, she has recycled that early pain into positive energy. She now celebrates the stand-out properties of her big hair. Now she treats it like a fabulous living canvas to express her personality. She enjoys playing around with its incredible density and volume, sometimes combing and fluffing it out into a wonderful big cloud around her face; sometimes decorating it lavishly. She loves the impact her hair can make and her fashion choices aim to complement the look of a woman who is totally 'in synch with her kink'. Sometimes revenge is not only sweet; it's also utterly inspirational.

In response to the CROWN Act in the US, the Halo Collective, an alliance of British organisations, is calling on schools and workplaces to adopt the Halo Code, the UK's first Black hair code created to protect those in schools and workplaces with natural hairstyles associated with racial, ethnic and cultural identities. Since its launch in December 2020, the Halo Code has been signed by more than five hundred UK companies.

Our natural hair is now coming back into its own. As we are learning more about the associated health risks, sales in relaxer treatments both in salons and on the shelves are at an all-time low. The resurgence of the natural hair movement has seen many Black women literally and figuratively 'going back to their roots' by styling their natural hair exactly as they want it, while maintaining the integrity of its texture. Today, there is already a generation of young women who have grown up free from relaxer dependency and who consider their natural hair as a vibrant expression of their personality and their identity. In resetting the cultural dial of Black hair, it seems that many Black women now have a better understanding and intimacy with their own hair, fully appreciating its intrinsic beauty and versatility. Others want to reclaim the lost relationship with their hair by undergoing the 'big chop'. This involves cutting off their relaxed hair to make way for the new growth of their natural curl. Some of these women are rediscovering their natural-grown hair for the first time in years, having relaxed it for so long that they had forgotten what it looked like. Whether for health reasons, environmental concerns or a new sense of empowerment in their Black identity, women are taking back control of their natural textured hair. It's as if they are saying, '*We'll* take it from here, thanks. *We'll* decide how we feel about it.'

And what about Black men? How do they feel about their natural hair? While theirs are not my stories to tell, I know that they too have plenty of experiences to share when it comes to hair-shaming and hair discrimination. But while few men in Britain have ever had to face the dilemma of chemically relaxing or straightening their hair, how important is their natural textured hair to their sense of self, well-being and the image they project today?

It seems that you don't have to look far for the answer.

While I'm no style historian, it's easy to see that a quiet revolution has been taking place on the top of the heads of Black men for some time now. Over the past twenty years in the UK, the interest in Black haircare and grooming for men has taken a turn for the creative and often playful, as celebrity influencers from the world of music and sport have given Black men a sense of the unique versatility of their natural-grown hair. For many, this has been a liberating initiative allowing them to view their hair as an adventure playground where they can express their individuality as well as their cultural heritage.

For lots of Black men, that regular trip to the barber's for the cursory short-crop, low-maintenance cut – the badge of conformity – is a thing of the past. Today, Black barbers have had to up their skills to provide precision cuts and fades that are often complemented by ice-pick sideburns or chin straps; and bleaching and dying, once seen as the choice of extroverts, has now become a common fashion choice, adding a different dimension to your look. No longer fearing the growth of their hair as they once may have done, men are opting to grow their hair longer and wear it in cornrows, locs, twists and a variety of braids. In an age when the expression 'self-care' is no longer loaded with feminine overtones, there is an increased interest and market for Black hair and skin products for men as part of their daily regimen to looking good.

There is no doubt that the world of football has had a big influence on how the fashionable Black man wears his hair today. It's on the football pitch that we see an impressive array of Black hairstyles regularly showcased; styles that are inspiring men to think differently about what their hair says about them and how they want to present themselves to the world. The natural dense texture of Afro hair lends itself to hard cuts and partings and fantastic geometric designs at the back and sides, a style we see on a lot of players who wear their hair like a badge of heritage. One of the more popular trends is the tapered fade at the front and sides with the high-top Afro, as worn by Jude Bellingham, Real Madrid and England football player. These men are active, alpha males sending out a joyful and prideful message about how they feel about their hair and how it's a big part of the positive image they want to project. Just look at what my hair can do! I love it and I'm going to let it say something about me!

Football and the hip-hop music scene, together with easy access to style tutorials on social media, are giving men more ideas to play with, and all the signs point to the fact that men are now fully realising the creative potential of their natural hair texture. That, like women, they have a complex and emotional attachment to it, which they may not have fully recognised before but which they are now eager to explore and invest in. The evolvement of

Black men's relationship with their hair deserves its own thorough investigation with proper research and in-depth studies, but in the spirit of personal enquiry, I couldn't resist conducting my own random vox pop whenever I got the chance.

When I run into Benjie buying his salad at M&S, his white mum joins in the discussion. She is the natural mother of three mixed-race boys and was glad to avoid the intensive hair rituals she knew would have been expected had they been girls. As children, she always maintained the boys' kinky hair with short cuts all round. But Benjie, in his twenties, is now wearing his hair high and wide in a prideful and impressive Afro. He confesses that he is taking care of and 'enjoying' his hair for the first time, saying, 'I wanted to take ownership of it, as it's a big part of my identity and what you immediately notice about me. I pick up all my haircare tips from the internet, including the best products to use. There's no excuse for men not knowing how to look after their own hair any more, it's all out there online.'

Supermarkets are fertile ground for impromptu chats and in Sainsbury's, I meet Kevin. He's in his forties and has long braids with a blue thread twisted into them. He grew up with sisters and went through the Sunday-night Black family ritual of bath-hair-wash-and-braiding. 'My father always braided my hair right up until I was into my thirties. Now I've learned to braid it myself, as it's too intimate and personal. I wear this protective style because I don't like people messing with it, barbers and such. The blue? I just felt like a change and I think it looks cool.'

I find Declan, a computer science student, working behind a popular bar in Leeds where I'd gone to catch up with a friend. Declan wears his hair in short even twists with a centre parting, a style that his girlfriend helps him maintain. He says, 'I saw other guys making a statement with their hair and I thought, why not? I feel as if more of my personality is out there now and people often comment on it. Men don't really talk much about their hair, do they? But I think, as we all get more creative with it, that's changing too. Hey, why jam a baseball cap on what could be your most outstanding asset?'

Dubem is Nigerian and he's been in the UK with his wife for a few years now. He's studying for an MA in health and social care. I see him getting onto the same bus as me, pushing a lady in a wheelchair. Dubem is wearing short braids caught up in a playful topknot on the crown of his head and I can't resist asking him about his style. He says, 'I used to be a bank manager back in Nigeria and I could never have worn my hair like this. Never! Back then, it was all about that professional cut-and-go look. Since coming to Britain, I've felt more liberated when it comes to expressing myself – *all* of myself. Now I can have more fun with it and my wife helps me experiment with new styles all the time.'

So while women, it seems, are often playing a part in their men's haircare, the men themselves are totally invested in it and are very clear about the look they want to achieve. They are also savvy about essential haircare products such as moisturising preparations to keep their hair healthy. Just like the women, they have gained confidence in their natural look; no longer toning themselves down to be that Black person who is 'easy on the eye'. Instead of trying to draw attention away from their most visible difference, with the all-purpose short back and sides, they are now highlighting and even flaunting its terrific versatility.

There's no doubt that today natural hair is coming back strong for both men and women. There's a new respect for its tough, springy texture and a pride and confidence in its many commutations, from ultra-stylish to dramatic. And as more women choose not to subdue its natural vitality with chemicals, we are seeing Black hair in all its transmutations going mainstream. We see it in the media in advertising, TV presenters and hi-vis celebrities, and we see it sliding down the catwalks on stunning fashion models. More recently, the world has got to see Black hair in its very own variety show with the women of Wakanda in the box-office sensation *Black Panther*. Fantasy women they may be, but the ingenious versatility of their hairstyles reflects their characters' growth, evolution and identity throughout the film; their hair stories are powerful metaphors for both female strength and vulnerability. But most of all, we see it in our high streets, from London to New York, where natural styles are being worn with a pride and panache as never before. Now it's a case of: how do I wear thee? Let me count the ways. And whether it's braids, Bantu knots, buzz cuts, twist-outs, puffs, space buns or sky-high pineapple ponytails and topknots, it's thrilling to see natural hair with its limitless variations being wholeheartedly embraced with such stylish confidence. No more understatement. No more apology. In wearing our natural hair, we are back in tune with our authentic selves as we embrace forsaken traditions and culture with renewed and creative vigour. And it's not just a passing phase. Not this time.

What's the big deal? It's just hair. Why make such a song and dance about it? We've heard this more than once and I'm sure we'll hear it many more times. The truth is that Afro hair is so much more than the spiral strands growing out of our scalp – and, by the way, it could definitely carry a musical with some memorable song-and-dance numbers.

This year will see the eighth anniversary of World Afro Day, a global day of celebration and liberation for Afro hair and identity. The day aims to recognise the beauty, history and significance of Afro hair and to eradicate the biases that have formed around it. Last year I spoke to a group of high school students on World Afro Day, and after my speech one of the students approached me: 'Wow! That was kinda like history, social studies, geography and art all rolled into one class.'

I couldn't have summed it up any better than that. Afro hair encompasses so much, and right now it's living its best life.

This hair. It holds our history, stores our memories and keeps our secrets; it tells our stories and speaks our truth. Charged and fizzling with its own energy, like Winnie-the-Pooh's Tigger, its bounce and spring can sometimes be hard to harness, but that's its feisty nature. It coils, it kinks, it twists – it's hair with attitude. It knows its own strength and sometimes it fights back. But like a complex circular maze, it offers so many different pathways to a deeper connection with who we are and where we have come from. We are Black women secure in our own beauty, standing on the shoulders of those whose stamina and instinct for survival provided a map of resilience and courage that signposts our future and fuels our creative fires. As we make peace with the shadows of the past, this hair, with all its endless amazing configurations, is a big part of our journey. It shapes our identity, projects our personality and has the power to ignite our imaginations into the stratosphere. This hair; it's our lasting, most intimate inheritance. Let's praise it like we should.

# ACKNOWLEDGEMENTS

For all the friends who encouraged and supported me with this project right from the start and who have watched it as it blossomed, know that you have been the following winds that helped keep me afloat and on course.

For their advice, contributions, willingness to read early drafts, and for their active interest in what became of me and the book, special thanks go to: Dr Alun Rees and Lisa Carruthers for their invaluable IT support and editorial advice, all served with plentiful cups of tea and cake; Anne Haynes, ex-civil-servant-in-arms, for helpful discussions on content and for being my tireless cheerleader; the Reverend Canon Michael Glanville-Smith and his wife Dai, who always backed me like a winner; Katie Albert, and others, who were happy to share their untold stories throughout the book; Adrian Lukis, actor and writer, whose love and encouragement, like Ronnie Laws on sax,